Kayla Lobermeier

*Creator of Under A Tin Roof™*

# The Prairie Kitchen Cookbook

75 Wholesome Heartland Recipes
*for* Every Season

PAGE STREET
PUBLISHING CO.

First published in 2023 by
Page Street Publishing Co.
27 Congress Street, Suite 1511
Salem, MA 01970
www.pagestreetpublishing.com

Distributed by Macmillan, sales in Canada by The Canadian Manda Group.

27  26  25  24  23     1  2  3  4  5

ISBN-13: 978-1-64567-989-9
ISBN-10: 1-64567-989-6

Library of Congress Control Number: 2022946826

Cover and book design by Rosie Stewart for Page Street Publishing Co.
Photography by Kayla Lobermeier, illustrations by Jill Haupt

Printed and bound in China

Page Street Publishing protects our planet by donating to nonprofits
like The Trustees, which focuses on local land conservation.

# ❦ *Dedication* ❦

To my family, you have never once doubted me and continually push me to greater heights. I am forever grateful to you for loving and believing in my passions and helping me follow my dreams.

To my children, may this book be held forever in your hearts as a special piece to pass down to your children and their children, a way to remember what Mom made for you when you were once little.

To my Under A Tin Roof readers, without you, this book would not exist. Thank you for following along my journey for the last decade, for reading daily, and for your support throughout every high and low. I am forever indebted to you!

# Table of Contents

# INTRODUCTION

## *My Story*

My story with food truly starts when I was at my lowest point. I had grown up in the Midwest, but my parents were then living in the suburbs of Houston, Texas. The original plan was to fly down to Texas to pack up a few more of my things before I moved in to my college dorm room. Instead, I came home with some unexpected news. I was inside a bathroom stall in an airport holding a positive pregnancy test that turned my entire world upside down. It was only a handful of days later that I realized I would be raising the baby on my own, with the help of my parents. I was 18 years old, unemployed, and had no idea what I was going to do next. I spent my entire pregnancy poring over research on how I could make the environment my baby was growing in healthful and helpful. It was then that I started teaching myself the art of cooking.

I had not spent much of my life cooking. In fact, I did not take an interest in cooking until I graduated high school. As a child, I spent the weekends baking cookies, cakes, and cream cheese–filled pumpkin rolls with my dad. I never realized that what we were doing was considered "from scratch." All I knew was that these were the recipes that had been passed down to him, and that it was our way to spend time together when he was home from work. For my first job, I worked as a waitress and kitchen helper at a small cafe and tearoom. It was there that I truly learned what it meant to cook food from scratch. The dishes were absolutely incredible, though the recipes were rather simple. Creamy chicken-and-dumpling soup, chicken salad with strawberries served on a croissant, and triple-layered chocolate cakes were all things that we served on the sweetest floral china plates. These were all meals that inspired me to try making my own recipes at home.

I wanted to learn to make everything myself, to nourish my body and my baby with the best food that I possibly could. I really have to give my son, who was born on a rainy morning in April, much of the credit for where my journey with food has led us both. Without him, I may never have taken the leap to make myself better and to try new things. Is that not how most stories begin?

As the years went by, I continued to create in the kitchen and discovered a deep love for the hobby. I stopped working in restaurants and began working with my mother, Jill. A graphic designer, she had owned her own creative business for more than 20 years. As our story goes, she needed help creating a website and online presence, and I needed a space to write my story. I started a blog, Under A Tin Roof™, in 2015, the same year my son was born, and began documenting our life and adventures as new homesteaders.

My parents, son, and I packed up and moved to rural southeast Iowa. It was a complete culture shock to my previous life in the city suburbs. The community was itty-bitty; it had only around 1,000 people, with almost half of the population being Old Order Amish. There were horses and buggies driving down the road, people working in their vegetable gardens, goats and ponies and chickens meandering about the pastures, roadside stands filled with pumpkins, and folks who would welcome you into the neighborhood with a warm casserole and apple pie. It was the most inspiring place that I had ever lived, and it felt as if I had just stepped into the love-child community of *Gilmore Girls* and *Little House on the Prairie*.

We spent our days perusing local greenhouses filled with flowers and vegetable starts, eating Amish donuts and butterhorns, and watching sheep and goats play in the pasture, all while learning where our food came from. I wrote about the little garden we grew in the backyard, where my dad built a greenhouse out of reclaimed glass windows with whitewashed wooden panes. We drove into town and bought a little box with six peeping, fluffy chicks inside, and we raised them until they laid beautiful brown and blue eggs. We planted apple trees and bought a beehive. The garden was growing so abundantly with produce that I had to figure out what to do with it all. By my own doing, I was forced into cooking seasonal meals and learning how to preserve my excess produce.

Eventually, we realized how much we absolutely loved being self-sufficient. It felt like freedom from all that had troubled us about a hustle-and-bustle lifestyle. Before, we had spent all our extra funds on dining out, home decor, and excessive amounts of clothing. It began to dawn on us how much happier and healthier we felt investing our lives into creating a homestead. We gave up all our commercialized lifestyle habits and bought a farm.

I have now been learning the art of homesteading, gardening, cooking from scratch, raising small livestock, and preserving our harvest for almost a decade. In all that time, I have shared our journey on my blog and helped others bring a small bit of that lifestyle to their own homes. There are so many things that have become second nature to me, a woman who had no previous knowledge nor formal training about cooking and baking, or about living a life inspired by old-fashioned skills. But it happened all the same.

## Why Prairie Cooking?

As my journey with food expanded, so did my interest in learning my family's personal history and the history of the region we now call home. Growing up, I had always had a love for romance- and period-inspired films, books, clothing, and home decor. The more I learned about cooking meals with whole food ingredients, the more the history of those dishes became important to me as well. Making a loaf of bread began to feel natural, as if I was somehow connecting through time to the people who formed my family in past generations, to the people who once lived on the prairies that surrounded our farm.

In 1853, my fourth great-grandfather, Ulrich Niffenegger, made his way from Bern, Switzerland, to Ohio and eventually settled his family in the state of Iowa. It was a territory that was different from anywhere the settlers had seen before, especially those coming from the eastern states. There were no forests or woodland animals, no mountains or mighty rivers and lakes. Rather, it was a land covered in tall Indian grass, black-eyed Susans, goldenrod, switchgrass, echinacea, spiderwort, and coreopsis. The fauna included white-tailed deer, cottontails, groundhogs, goldfinches, prairie rattlesnakes, bald eagles, red-tailed hawks, and walleye. The times were difficult, often unfortunate for many, as they built their farms from the ground up, with little to no supplies. However, the rewards far outweighed the pains. It took little time for the early settlers to learn about the richness of the soil that they had set foot upon and to discover the incredible wildlife that would help to feed their families.

For me, prairie cooking is only natural. It is the food of my family, of my ancestors. My personal heritage is built around the cultures in Germany, Sweden, Denmark, Poland, Switzerland, England, and Scotland. Just like the people who settled on the land that I now call home and that my family has called home for almost 200 years, I cannot help but feel the connection toward the traditions that were made and served at the supper table.

In this book, you will find recipes that are rooted deep in tradition and reminiscent of those you might find in an old book of cookery from the late eighteenth and nineteenth centuries, though these recipes have a modern twist. From homemade crusty breads and savory stews to roast turkeys and rustic berry pies, you will find something that brings about memories of an old-fashioned life. My hope is that, with this cookbook, you may find a love of from-scratch cooking for yourself. Whether you have cooked for your family for years or have never made anything that does not come in a box, with this book you will be able to create incredibly wholesome and hearty meals for the special people in your life. If anything, you can walk away knowing that real food is still here, and that it is good and whole and full of flavor.

Settle in for a while with me, to live a slow and simple lifestyle through the seasons.

*Kayla Lobermeier*

# A FARMER'S BREAKFAST

On the farm, the day begins at dawn. There are animals that must be fed and led out to the pasture, eggs to be collected, and gardens to be watered and tended to. While the rest of the world sleeps, the farmer is up and about at work. With the experience of growing vegetables for a community-supported agriculture program, and now flowers for our neighbors, I am no stranger to the hunger that comes after the toilsome hours of beginning hard labor at daybreak. Our breakfast is typically enjoyed in the later morning hours, when the children finally rise from sleep, and there are many hungry mouths to feed in our home.

Breakfast is my favorite meal of the day. I love filling up early, then slowly dwindling my portions throughout the day. This is something that my family has always done, even before we became Iowa farmers. A good and hearty breakfast was made with scrambled or fried eggs, hashed potatoes, sausage and bacon, and a piece of toast slathered with butter. While this sounds like the perfect country breakfast, all the components of that meal came premade from the store. Now, I make all of it from scratch, with ingredients that we either grow or raise ourselves, and what a journey it took to get there! My kitchen looks like something out of the old world, but that is what I love most about it.

In this chapter, I hope that you are able to enjoy a taste of our country breakfast scene. You will find a wonderful mixture of sweet and savory dishes—such as Pumpkin Butter Waffles with Whipped Maple Bourbon Butter (page 13), Sweet Marjoram- and Nutmeg-Spiced Breakfast Sausage (page 17), and Chicken-Fried Sirloin Steak (page 32)—that are sure to leave you feeling as if you've just sat down at our long wooden farm table, which is filled with little bowls of mulberries and cherry tomatoes and cups of hot coffee. You'll feel the warm breeze coming in through the window and smell the fresh flowers from the field. Above all, these recipes give you the opportunity to make it all from scratch, too!

# Pumpkin Butter Waffles with Whipped Maple Bourbon Butter

Is there anything better than a pumpkin waffle? Try making a batch with spiced pumpkin butter, and I think that you may have your answer! In the autumn, when it is time to harvest the pumpkins, I love turning the velvety rich flesh into my homemade pumpkin butter. Pumpkin butter is a reduced pumpkin puree, cooked over the stove with warm autumnal spices, such as cinnamon, allspice, nutmeg, and cloves, and sweetened with maple syrup and brown sugar. It's everything that you love about a pumpkin pie and perfect for mixing into baked goods or spreading over your next batch of pancakes. These waffles are made up of everything that I love about fall. The addition of an incredibly rich whipped Maple Bourbon Butter makes them all the more irresistible.

## SERVES 4

### Pumpkin Butter Waffles

2 cups (250 g) all-purpose flour

2 tsp (8 g) baking powder

1 tsp ground cinnamon

¼ cup (50 g) granulated sugar

2 tbsp (28 g) packed brown sugar

½ tsp kosher salt

4 large eggs

1½ cups (360 ml) whole milk

8 oz (226 g) pumpkin butter

½ cup (120 ml) melted salted butter

1 tsp vanilla extract

### Maple Bourbon Butter

4 tbsp (56 g) salted butter, softened

2 tsp (10 ml) maple syrup

1 tsp bourbon

Pinch of fine sea salt

### For Serving

Pure maple syrup

For the waffles, in a large bowl, mix together the flour, baking powder, cinnamon, granulated sugar, brown sugar, and salt. Add the eggs, milk, pumpkin butter, melted butter, and vanilla, and mix until the ingredients are just combined.

Preheat a waffle iron. Spray it with cooking spray or brush it with melted butter. Pour 1 cup (240 ml) of the batter onto the waffle iron, adjusting the amount as needed for the size of your waffle iron, and cook the waffles for 4 to 6 minutes, or until they are golden brown. Repeat with the rest of the waffle batter.

For the Maple Bourbon Butter, in a small bowl, whip together the butter, maple syrup, bourbon, and salt. Serve the hot waffles with the Maple Bourbon Butter and maple syrup.

 TIP: If you cannot make your own homemade pumpkin butter, some major chain and many specialty grocery stores carry pumpkin butter seasonally. Another option is to buy it online!

# Any Berry Baked Oatmeal

While I love to make a big country breakfast most mornings, there are many days when something quick, delicious, and healthy is the option that sounds best. My children love oatmeal for breakfast, and one of my favorite ways to make it is baked and filled with fruit. Full of texture and sweetness, this oatmeal is a simple and filling breakfast that you can have ready in less than an hour. This is pictured with blueberries, strawberries, and blackberries, but it can be made with practically any fruit that is in season. I love it best with strawberries and blueberries, but for a more autumnal vibe, make it with chopped apples or late-season peaches.

## SERVES 6

2 cups (180 g) rolled oats

½ cup (112 g) packed brown sugar

1 tsp ground cinnamon

¼ tsp kosher salt

2 large eggs, lightly beaten

¼ cup (60 ml) maple syrup

4 tbsp (60 ml) melted salted butter

1½ cups (360 ml) whole milk

2 cups (150 g) chopped fresh fruit: strawberries, blueberries, blackberries, raspberries, peaches, apples, etc., divided, plus more for serving

Heavy cream, optional

Preheat the oven to 375°F (190°C). Grease a 9 x 13–inch (23 x 33–cm) casserole dish and set it aside.

In a large bowl, combine the oats, brown sugar, cinnamon, and salt. Mix in the brown sugar with your fingers to evenly disperse the sugar crystals. Add the eggs, maple syrup, butter, and milk to the oat mixture, and stir it with a rubber spatula. Once it's fully combined, stir in 1 cup (75 g) of the fruit.

Evenly spread the oatmeal into the prepared baking dish. Arrange the remaining 1 cup (75 g) of fruit on top of the oatmeal in a pattern of your choosing. Bake the oatmeal for 35 to 40 minutes, or until the liquid has been soaked up by the oats. Allow the oatmeal to rest for 5 minutes before slicing it.

Serve the oatmeal warm, topped with more fresh fruit and the heavy cream, if desired.

# Sweet Marjoram- and Nutmeg-Spiced Breakfast Sausage

This is my absolute favorite way to season sausage. It is both savory and sweet, making it a perfect combination for breakfast, though it works for several dishes. This is a true Heartland-style seasoning blend, one that I find unique to the German and Dutch heritage around our sleepy farm town. I have found in my journey of cooking prairie meals that the secret ingredient is always nutmeg. With a spicy, sweet, peppery flavor, it brings gusto to most dishes in which you would not necessarily include it. I love it as my own secret ingredient, because I think it gives recipes an old-fashioned feeling. We love to serve this sausage fresh for the breakfast table, but it also works if you would rather turn it into cased sausage links or a uniquely flavored brat!

SERVES 6

2 lb (908 g) 80/20 ground pork, cold

2 tsp (2 g) minced fresh parsley

2 tsp (12 g) kosher salt

1 tsp dried sage

1 tsp dried marjoram

1 tsp chili powder

1 tsp smoked paprika

1 tsp ground black pepper

½ tsp onion powder

½ tsp ground white pepper

¼ tsp dried thyme

¼ tsp ground nutmeg

2 tsp (10 ml) cooking oil or (5 g) lard

In a large bowl, mix together the pork, parsley, salt, sage, marjoram, chili powder, paprika, black pepper, onion powder, white pepper, thyme, and nutmeg, using your hands. To evenly flavor the sausage, make sure the seasoning blend is well incorporated throughout the meat. Divide the mixture in half and shape each half into a 6-inch (15-cm)-long log. Wrap each log in plastic wrap, and refrigerate the logs for several hours, or up to overnight.

When you are ready to cook the sausage, line a plate with paper towels. Cut the logs into 1-inch (2.5-cm)-thick slices. Keep the meat cold before frying it. Heat the oil in a skillet over medium-high heat until it shimmers, about 2 minutes. Fry the sausage patties for about 3 minutes on each side, pressing gently on them after flipping them, or until they have reached 160°F (71°C) on an instant-read thermometer inserted into the center. Place the slices on the prepared plate to drain the fat, and serve them hot.

# Perfect Blueberry Streusel Muffins with Variations

On mornings when I have little time to make an extravagant breakfast, I whip up a batch of muffins and send them off in a cloth napkin with everyone as they head out the door. I love how versatile this muffin recipe is: It's easily transformed into a summer sensation with fresh blueberries or strawberries, or a perfectly decadent dessert with dark chocolate. They are incredibly soft and moist, making them an easy family favorite. You will love them for any occasion and will surely be bringing them with you to your next morning coffee date!

## MAKES 12 STANDARD OR 6 JUMBO MUFFINS

### Muffin Base
2¼ cups (282 g) all-purpose flour

2 tsp (8 g) baking powder

½ tsp baking soda

½ tsp kosher salt

1 cup (200 g) granulated sugar

½ cup (120 ml) vegetable oil or melted butter

1 cup (240 ml) sour cream

2 large eggs

1 tsp vanilla extract

### Fruit-Filled Muffins
1 cup (75 g) chopped fresh fruit: blueberries, raspberries, peaches, strawberries, rhubarb, apple, etc.

2 tbsp (30 ml) freshly squeezed lemon juice

Coarse sugar

### Chocolate Chunk Muffins
1 cup (168 g) semisweet milk chocolate chips

½ cup (84 g) chunked dark chocolate

Coarse sugar

### Streusel-Topped Muffins
4 tbsp (60 ml) melted salted butter

½ cup (63 g) all-purpose flour

½ cup (100 g) granulated sugar

1 tsp ground cinnamon

Preheat the oven to 375°F (190°C). Grease or lightly spray a 12-cup or 6-cup jumbo muffin tin with cooking spray and set it aside.

For the Muffin Base, in a large mixing bowl, combine the flour, baking powder, baking soda, salt, and sugar. Add the oil, sour cream, eggs, and vanilla.

For Fruit-Filled Muffins, gently fold in the fruit and lemon juice with a spatula.

For the chocolate muffins, gently fold in the chocolate chips and dark chocolate with a spatula.

Divide the batter evenly between the muffin cups, filling them about two-thirds full. Dust the muffins with coarse sugar; if you are topping the muffins with streusel, skip this step.

If you are topping the muffins with streusel, mix together the butter, flour, sugar, and cinnamon in a small bowl. Top the muffins with the streusel, and gently press it into the batter.

Bake the muffins for 25 to 30 minutes, or until the muffins are golden brown on top and a toothpick inserted into the center comes out clean. Allow the muffins to sit in the tin for 5 minutes, then move them to a wire rack to cool.

# White-Peppered Pork Sausage Gravy

I cannot think of any recipe more suited to farm life on the prairie than biscuits and gravy! This is a meal that we often eat at any time of the day, though we prefer it as a hearty breakfast before heading out to weed the garden, to chore the animals, or work in the cut flower field. It works as a quick supper, too, on days when life becomes a bit too hectic for a meal that needs several hours to plan ahead and prepare. With experience, one can whip up a helping of biscuits and gravy in less than an hour! I love this gravy, with its addition of a seasoned pork sausage. I usually use breakfast sausage, but Italian sausage works wonderfully as well. If you prefer to eat this meatless, it tastes just as delicious. The gravy can be used for all sorts of dishes, so have fun with it! This recipe uses a basic béchamel-style gravy or sauce, which is one recipe that all cooks should learn.

## SERVES 4

½ lb (226 g) Sweet Marjoram- and Nutmeg-Spiced Breakfast Sausage (page 17)

4 tbsp (56 g) salted butter

¼ cup (32 g) all-purpose flour

2 cups (480 ml) whole milk, divided

½ tsp kosher salt

½ tsp ground black pepper

½ tsp ground white pepper

Big Buttermilk Biscuits, for serving (page 143)

In a large skillet over medium-high heat, cook the sausage for 7 to 10 minutes, or until it's browned, crumbling the meat into fine pieces as you stir. Drain the fat, and set the sausage aside.

In a medium saucepan, melt the butter over medium heat. Whisk in the flour to create a roux. Cook the mixture until the roux has lightly browned and smells a bit nutty, 2 to 3 minutes.

Slowly begin to pour in the milk, 1 cup (240 ml) at a time. Whisk in the first cup (240 ml) until the mixture begins to boil and thicken, 3 to 5 minutes. Add the second cup (240 ml) of milk in a similar fashion, whisking constantly until the gravy comes to a boil and thickens. Stir in the salt, black pepper, and white pepper, then adjust the seasonings to taste.

Remove the gravy from the heat, and stir in the cooked sausage. Cover the gravy until you are ready to serve it, to prevent a thin skin from forming on top of the gravy. Serve the gravy warm, with the biscuits. The gravy can be refrigerated in a container with an airtight lid for about 1 week.

# Garden Tomato, Basil, and Bacon Tart

There is nothing quite like enjoying a tomato fresh off the vine, ripened by the sun and sweetened in the heat of summer. With this dish, I was inspired by an old summer kitchen, where leafy greens were ground into pesto and fresh milk was turned into soft cheeses. This tart allows you to enjoy all those flavors in accompaniment with fresh basil pesto and creamy mozzarella cheese. Easy to whip up in a jiffy, this tart has a delightful no-bake filling that is perfect for a refreshingly simple summer dish to share!

## SERVES 6

Single Crisp and Flaky Pie Crust (page 151)

1 tbsp (4 g) finely chopped fresh rosemary

1 tbsp (2 g) fresh thyme leaves

6 slices bacon

4 oz (112 g) cream cheese

½ cup (56 g) shredded fresh mozzarella

1 tsp kosher salt

1 tsp ground black pepper

½ cup (120 ml) basil pesto, divided

2 tbsp (30 ml) balsamic vinegar

1 tbsp (15 ml) olive oil

1 lb (454 g) heirloom tomatoes, sliced ¼ inch (6 mm) thick

Flaky sea salt, for serving

Freshly cracked black pepper, for serving

Fresh basil leaves, for serving

Begin by making the pie crust according to the directions on page 151. To the dry ingredients, add the rosemary and thyme. Continue as directed, then refrigerate the dough for at least 1 hour before using it.

Preheat the oven to 400°F (200°C), and line a plate with paper towels.

On a lightly floured surface, roll the dough into a 12-inch (30-cm) circle. With the edge of the dough, wrap it around your rolling pin and gently roll the dough to fully wrap around the rolling pin. Hold the rolling pin above a 10-inch (25-cm) tart pan, with the visible edge of the dough near the edge of the pan. Unroll the dough and press it into the bottom and edges of the pan. Trim off the top of the dough so that it lines up with the edge of the pan. Prick the bottom of the crust all over with a fork. Line the crust with parchment paper, fill it with pie weights, and bake the crust for 20 minutes. Remove the weights and parchment paper, and bake the crust for 5 to 10 minutes, or until it's just lightly browned. Set the pie crust aside to cool.

In a skillet, cook the bacon over medium-high heat for 2 to 3 minutes per side, or until it's lightly crisped. Place the bacon on the prepared plate to drain the fat and set aside the plate.

In a medium bowl, mix the cream cheese, mozzarella, salt, pepper, and ¼ cup (60 ml) of the pesto until the mixture is smooth and creamy. In a small bowl, mix together the remaining ¼ cup (60 ml) of pesto, balsamic vinegar, and olive oil.

Spread the cheese mixture in the bottom of the baked tart crust until it's smooth and level. Top the cheese mixture with the tomato slices; layering a few tomatoes is perfectly fine. Drizzle the top with the pesto–vinegar mixture. For serving, sprinkle the sea salt, cracked pepper, and basil over the tart.

# Cinnamon Walnut Butterhorns

You cannot visit an Amish community without trying a butterhorn, which is similar to a crescent roll. This homemade version is light, buttery, and absolutely scrumptious! An eighteenth-century invention, nut horns are a puffy bread dough with butter brushed on, cut into the shape of pie pieces, and rolled up. A Jewish pastry, called *rugelach*, is sometimes called a *nut horn*, as many recipes include walnuts and preserves in the center. For breakfast, I like to make a classic butterhorn recipe that invites a little bit more to the palate. With brown sugar, cinnamon, and walnuts, you sense that you are having something quite fancy for your breakfast roll, though it takes little effort to make.

## MAKES 24 ROLLS

4½–5 cups (563–625 g) all-purpose flour, divided

2 tbsp (24 g) active dry yeast

1½ tsp (4 g) ground cinnamon, divided

1 cup (240 ml) whole milk

½ cup (112 g) packed brown sugar

½ tsp fine sea salt

½ cup (112 g) butter

2 large eggs

⅓ cup (66 g) granulated sugar

½ cup (44 g) finely chopped walnuts

¼ cup (60 ml) melted salted butter, divided

Lightly grease a large bowl, and set it aside.

In a standing electric mixer fitted with a dough hook, combine 2 cups (250 g) of the flour, the yeast, and ½ teaspoon of the cinnamon. You can also make this dough by hand by adding the ingredients to a large bowl. Set aside the mixture.

In small saucepan, whisk together the milk, brown sugar, and salt. Add the butter and warm the mixture over medium heat, until the butter begins to melt, at about 120°F (50°C) on an instant-read thermometer. Remove the pan from the heat, and pour the liquid mixture into the flour mixture. Add the eggs.

Begin to mix the dough over medium-high speed in the electric mixer or by hand with a wooden spoon until the ingredients are well combined. Slowly incorporate the remainder of the flour, or as much of it as you can, until a soft and smooth dough begins to form, about 10 minutes with an electric mixer. If making the dough by hand, begin kneading in the remaining flour until the dough is no longer shaggy, but smooth and elastic, 15 to 20 minutes. The dough should no longer cling to the sides of the bowl, but it will still be a bit sticky, soft, and easily pliable. If it is too stiff and dry from too much flour, it will not rise. Place the dough in the greased bowl, and cover it with a damp towel or a large plate. Allow the dough to rise in a warm place until it's doubled in size, about 1 hour.

Meanwhile, in a small dish, combine the granulated sugar, remaining 1 teaspoon cinnamon, and the walnuts. Set aside the dish.

*(continued)*

# Cinnamon Walnut Butterhorns (Continued)

Line two baking sheets with parchment paper.

Gently deflate the dough with your hands, and turn it out onto a lightly floured surface. Divide the dough into two equal-sized pieces. Roll one-half of the dough into a 12-inch (30-cm) circle. Brush it with half of the melted butter, and sprinkle it with the walnut mixture.

With a pastry cutter or sharp knife, slice the dough into twelve wedges, much like cutting a round pizza. With the wider end of the triangle, roll the dough toward the point. Pinch the seam together. Place the pieces on the prepared baking sheets. Repeat with the other half of the dough.

Cover the finished rolls with a damp towel or plastic wrap, and let them rise until they are almost doubled in size and puffy, about 30 minutes. While the rolls are rising, preheat the oven to 375°F (190°C). Bake the rolls for 14 to 16 minutes, or until they are lightly golden.

TIP: With butterhorns, the dough can become quite dense rather quickly, so be sure to watch your flour additions, making sure the dough is still a bit wet and stretchy for its first rise. Wait until the shaped rolls have truly puffed during the rise before baking them. On a chilly day, sometimes it helps the butterhorns to rise if you preheat your oven to 200°F (100°C), place the trays on top of the oven, and slightly crack open the oven door. This gives them some extra warmth.

# Brioche Cinnamon Wreath Bread with Cream Cheese Icing

For years, my early mornings would be spent in the kitchen, with the scent of freshly baked cinnamon rolls wafting up the stairs. I would load the freshly frosted rolls into the back of our car and tote them off to the farmers' market. With so many pans of cinnamon rolls going in and out of our farmhouse, I found that experimenting with different types of doughs gave me a fun challenge. Brioche is an enriched dough made with lots of butter, eggs, and milk. The addition of these ingredients creates a pillowy soft crumb, which is further enhanced by an overnight cold proofing. This cinnamon roll recipe results in the softest rolls I have ever made. You may bake a wreath as pictured, or slice the dough into twelve individual rolls.

SERVES 6

### Brioche Sweet Dough

1 cup (240 ml) warm whole milk

2 tbsp (24 g) active dry yeast

¼ cup (50 g) granulated sugar

5 large eggs

1 tsp fine sea salt

6 cups (750 g) all-purpose flour

1 cup (224 g) salted butter, softened and cubed

For the dough, lightly grease a large bowl and set it aside.

In the bowl of a standing electric mixer fitted with a dough hook, whisk together the milk, yeast, and sugar. Let the mixture sit for about 5 minutes, or until the yeast blooms or grows a bit and becomes foamy. Whisk in the eggs and salt. Alternately, you may make this dough by hand by mixing the ingredients in a large bowl.

Begin to incorporate the flour, on low speed, or with a wooden spoon if you are making the dough by hand, until it forms a thick and sticky dough. Once all of the flour has been incorporated, slowly add in the butter a little bit at a time, incorporating it into the dough before adding the next pieces. Turn the mixer up to medium-high speed and knead the dough for 10 to 15 minutes, or until it becomes stronger and pulls away from the sides of the bowl. Brioche dough requires more time mixing or kneading, which creates a soft and stretchy dough. The dough should be strong enough to stretch thinly without breaking. By hand, this may take 20 to 25 minutes of kneading.

Form the dough into a ball with your hands and place it in the prepared bowl. Cover it with plastic wrap or a large plate, and let it rise at room temperature for about 2 hours, or until it's doubled in size. Punch down the dough, stretching it gently and shaping it into a ball again. Place it back in the same bowl, and cover it with plastic wrap or a large plate. Refrigerate the bowl for 8 to 12 hours or overnight.

*(continued)*

# Brioche Cinnamon Wreath Bread with Cream Cheese Icing (Continued)

## Cinnamon Filling

6 tbsp (84 g) salted butter, softened

1 cup (224 g) packed brown sugar

1 tbsp (8 g) ground cinnamon

## Cream Cheese Icing

4 oz (112 g) cream cheese, softened

2 cups (240 g) sifted powdered sugar

¼ cup (60 ml) whole milk or heavy cream

1 tsp (5 ml) vanilla extract

Pinch of fine sea salt

In the morning, remove the dough from the refrigerator. Pull it away from the sides of the bowl and onto a lightly floured work surface. Roll out the dough to a 12 x 16–inch (30 x 40–cm) rectangle.

For the filling, spread the butter over the dough. Sprinkle it evenly with the brown sugar and cinnamon. Roll up the dough lengthwise, starting from the longest side and working left to right. You will end up with a 16-inch (40-cm) log.

If you are making individual cinnamon rolls, grease a 9 x 13–inch (23 x 33–cm) pan. Slice the log into twelve equal-sized pieces with a sharp knife. Keep the rolls as tight as possible, adjusting if needed. Place the rolls in the prepared pan, cut side down, and cover them with plastic wrap or a damp kitchen towel. Let the rolls rise until puffed, about 40 minutes.

If you are making a wreath, line a large baking sheet with parchment paper. Slice the entire log down the center, lengthwise, to form two halves. Pinch the ends of the halves together at the top, then braid the halves together. Pinch the bottom ends of the halves together, then form the dough into a circle. Place the wreath on the baking sheet, and cover it with plastic wrap or a damp kitchen towel. Let the wreath rise until the dough is puffed, about 40 minutes.

Meanwhile, preheat the oven to 350°F (180°C). Bake the rolls for 30 to 35 minutes or the wreath for 35 to 40 minutes, or until it's lightly browned on the top. To test the rolls for doneness, use a paring knife to gently pull apart the innermost roll and look for any stickiness or dough that looks raw; the final rolls should be browned and firm when pressed. Let the rolls cool for 10 to 15 minutes before icing them.

To make the icing, whip together the cream cheese, powdered sugar, milk, vanilla, and salt for about 5 minutes, or until the mixture reaches the consistency of molasses. Drizzle the icing over the rolls or wreath, and serve them warm.

# Potato, Sausage, and Red Pepper Hash

When I was 18 years old, my family packed up our entire house and moved from the suburbs of Chicago, Illinois, to Houston, Texas. I had lived in the Midwest for my entire life up until that point, and it was down south that I discovered an entirely new food culture. As Houston is rather close to Louisiana, there were plenty of restaurants influenced by Cajun-style foods. There was a little cafe nearby that I loved. It served skillet-fried hashed potatoes with spicy Cajun sausage and sweet red peppers. It was the perfect blend of spiciness and starch, giving me a new look at how breakfast potatoes could be served. These potatoes are inspired by that delicious skillet I had long ago, during my short stay in the Southern Heartland.

## SERVES 4

*2 large russet potatoes, peeled and cut into ½-inch (1.3-cm) chunks*

*2 tbsp (14 g) lard or (30 ml) olive oil*

*1 small onion, diced*

*3 cloves garlic, minced*

*1 medium red bell pepper, diced*

*1 tsp smoked paprika*

*1 tsp kosher salt*

*½ tsp ground black pepper*

*Pinch of cayenne pepper*

*½ lb (226 g) kielbasa sausage, sliced into ½-inch (1.3-cm) rounds*

*2 tbsp (8 g) chopped fresh parsley, for serving*

In a large pot, cover the potatoes with water, and bring the water to a boil. Boil the potatoes for 10 minutes to soften them slightly. Drain the potatoes and set them aside.

In a large skillet, heat the lard over medium heat. Add the onion, garlic, and bell pepper, and cook the vegetables for 5 to 7 minutes, or until they are soft. Stir in the paprika, salt, black pepper, and cayenne. Add the sausage, and stir it in until the sausage is just warmed. Add the potatoes, and stir to coat them in the hot fat. Cook the hash until the potatoes are crispy and golden, about 8 minutes. Season with more salt and pepper, if desired.

Remove the hash from the heat and garnish it with the parsley, for serving.

# Chicken-Fried Sirloin Steak

A dish with German and Austrian origins, the chicken-fried steak comes from the southern states, though it is a recipe born from the classic wiener schnitzel. This dish is generally made with a tougher cut of meat, such as a round steak, but I like to make mine with sirloin for a truly tender and juicy bite. Historically, chicken-fried steak was made with breadcrumbs. This steak has a more modern feel to it, as it's leavened with baking powder and baking soda to bring about a nice puff after it's fried. This is a flavorsome breading that makes an excellent savory addition to the breakfast table.

## SERVES 4

2 (1-lb [454-g]) sirloin steaks

2 tsp (6 g) seasoned salt

¾ cup (94 g) all-purpose flour

½ tsp kosher salt

½ tsp ground black pepper

1 tsp smoked paprika

¼ tsp onion powder

¼ tsp baking powder

¼ tsp baking soda

Pinch of cayenne pepper

1 cup (240 ml) buttermilk

1 large egg

Salt and freshly ground black pepper

1 cup (240 ml) vegetable oil or (224 g) lard, for frying

White-Peppered Pork Sausage Gravy (page 21), for serving

Fried eggs, for serving

Remove the steaks from the refrigerator, pat them dry with paper towels, and sprinkle them all over with the seasoned salt.

Meanwhile, in a large flat dish such as a casserole dish or pie pan, whisk together the flour, kosher salt, pepper, paprika, onion powder, baking powder, baking soda, and cayenne. In a separate flat dish, whisk together the buttermilk and egg. Season the egg mixture with the salt and pepper.

Dredge the steaks in the flour mixture, coating them all over. Then, dip the coated steaks in the egg mixture. Dredge the steaks once more in the flour mixture, and set them on a plate. Cover the steaks with plastic wrap, and refrigerate them for 30 minutes.

Heat the oil in a large, deep skillet, at least 2 inches (5 cm) deep, to 375°F (190°C); use a candy thermometer to measure the oil temperature. Fry the steaks for about 3 minutes per side, or until they register 145°F (63°C) on an instant-read thermometer for medium rare.

Top the hot steaks with the gravy, and serve them alongside the fried eggs.

 TIP: The trick to keeping the flaky breading on the steak is to refrigerate it for about 30 minutes after the coating is applied.

# Prairie Pumpkin Scones with Maple Glaze

I must admit that, in the autumn months, I love anything made with pumpkin. It feels like a warm hug and delicious reward after many months spent working in the garden to grow the pumpkins themselves. Now that we grow, harvest, and preserve our own winter squash, I find that we eat pumpkin almost all year round! It is so easy to make and store pumpkin puree in the freezer, and I like to pull it out during the winter and early spring months to make these scones to enjoy on a chilly morning with a hot cup of coffee. These scones are soft, perfectly spiced, and topped with a delicious warm Maple Glaze. They can be made with any type of winter squash puree, if you would like to change it up now and again!

## SERVES 12

### Pumpkin Scones

2⅓ cups (292 g) all-purpose flour

¾ cup (150 g) granulated sugar

1 tsp ground cinnamon

½ tsp baking powder

½ tsp baking soda

½ tsp fine sea salt

¼ tsp ground nutmeg

¼ tsp ground ginger

½ cup (112 g) salted butter, cold and cubed

½ cup (114 g) pumpkin puree

¼ cup (60 ml) buttermilk

1 large egg

Milk, for brushing

Coarse sugar, for dusting

### Maple Glaze

1 cup (120 g) powdered sugar

½ tsp ground cinnamon

1 tbsp (15 ml) maple syrup

1 tbsp (15 ml) whole milk

For the scones, in a large bowl, combine the flour, sugar, cinnamon, baking powder, baking soda, salt, nutmeg, and ginger. Whisk until the ingredients are thoroughly combined. Cut in the butter with a pastry blender or fork until the mixture creates coarse crumbs about the size of a pea.

Add the pumpkin, buttermilk, and egg. Combine the pumpkin mixture and flour mixture with a wooden spoon, and eventually your hands, until a soft dough is formed. Do not over-knead the dough; it should no longer have any dry bits in it, even if it is a bit shaggy. Cover the dough with plastic wrap, and refrigerate it for 30 minutes.

Preheat the oven to 425°F (220°C), and line a baking sheet with parchment paper.

Press or roll out the dough to about ½ inch (1.3 cm) thick. Cut out the scones in any shape you like, such as with a round biscuit cutter or into diamonds with a sharp knife. Place the scones on the prepared baking sheet, spaced evenly. Brush them with the milk, and sprinkle them with the coarse sugar. Bake the scones for about 15 minutes, or until they are lightly golden. Cool the scones completely on a wire cooling rack before icing them.

To make the glaze, in a small bowl, mix together the powdered sugar, cinnamon, maple syrup, and milk. Drizzle the icing over the scones, then sprinkle them with more coarse sugar.

# Cranberry Brie and Walnut Pinwheels

Flaky puff pastry, melted Brie cheese, crunchy walnuts, and sweet cranberries make these an instant hit at any breakfast table. I love them for a holiday spread with baked eggs, hashed potatoes, and thick-cut bacon. They are a sweet little treat that brings people back for more, and everyone always loves these when I entertain! For something sweet with a bit of savory tang from the Brie, you cannot go wrong with these pleasant little pastry bites. They also make an excellent sweet appetizer.

SERVES 6

1 portion Easy Puff Pastry
(page 152) or 1 sheet frozen
puff pastry

2 tbsp (30 ml) melted salted butter

½ cup (44 g) chopped walnuts

½ cup (60 g) dried cranberries

4 oz (112 g) Brie, rind removed

3 tbsp (45 ml) honey, plus more for
serving, optional

Preheat the oven to 425°F (220°C). Line a baking sheet with parchment paper.

On a lightly floured surface, roll out the puff pastry dough, if homemade, to about a 12 x 16–inch (30 x 40–cm) rectangle. Brush the pastry with the butter. Sprinkle the walnuts and cranberries evenly over the dough. Place the Brie in a similar fashion, tearing it into small pieces. Drizzle the honey over the cheese.

Using the long end, roll up the dough similarly to a cinnamon roll dough. Start at one end and move along the entire edge, like a typewriter, rolling as tightly as possible, until the seam is on the bottom. With a sharp knife, slice the roll into ½-inch (1.3-cm)-thick pieces.

Place the pinwheels on the prepared baking sheet, about 2 inches (5 cm) apart, and bake them for 20 to 25 minutes, or until the puff pastry is golden brown and crisp. Rest the pinwheels on a wire rack until they are cool enough to handle. Drizzle them with more honey, if desired, and serve.

# Farmers' Market Buttermilk Donuts

Making donuts was something that I always wanted to try, but it took a long time before I built up the courage to do so. Deep-frying seemed like such a difficult feat to me. It surprised me how much fun this cooking method is! These donuts are reminiscent of a freshly baked Amish donut, and they are just as soft and melt-in-your-mouth worthy as a Krispy Kreme®. I have sold so many of these in our little farm store that I could probably fill up the entire shop with them! The donut itself has a long and complicated history, but one thing that I love about old-fashioned recipes for this fried cake is the addition of nutmeg and buttermilk, and sometimes even mashed potatoes. This particular recipe incorporates the acidic taste of buttermilk and spicy sweetness of ground nutmeg to create a lovely, old-world flavor.

## SERVES 6

### Buttermilk Donuts
2 tsp (8 g) active dry yeast

⅓ cup + 1 tsp (72 g) granulated sugar

1¼ cups (300 ml) warm buttermilk

4 tbsp (56 g) salted butter, softened

2 large eggs

1 tsp vanilla extract

1 tsp fine sea salt

¼ tsp nutmeg

4–5 cups (500–625 g) all-purpose flour

2 quarts (2 L) oil or (1.8 kg) lard

For the donuts, lightly grease a bowl for the donut dough, and flour a surface well or line a baking sheet with parchment paper.

In a large bowl or a standing electric mixer fitted with a dough hook, combine the yeast, sugar, and buttermilk. Allow the yeast to bloom, or to grow and become bubbly, for 5 to 7 minutes.

Add the butter, eggs, vanilla, salt, and nutmeg, and whisk to combine. Begin to slowly incorporate the flour, 1 cup (125 g) at a time, until a sticky dough forms. This dough is particularly soft and rather sticky, but it should not be completely wet. Add more or less flour as needed. If you are using an electric mixer, this will take 6 to 8 minutes, or 8 to 10 minutes by hand.

With wet hands, place the dough into the greased bowl. Cover it with plastic wrap or a large plate and place it in a warm spot until it's doubled in size, about 1 hour.

Gently deflate the dough with your hands and roll it out to about ½ inch (1.3 cm) thick. Cut out the dough with a 2-inch (5-cm) donut or biscuit cutter. Place the donuts on the well-floured surface or parchment-lined baking sheet, and cover them with a damp towel or plastic wrap. In a warm place, let the donuts rise for 15 to 25 minutes, or until they puff slightly; the amount of time depends on the temperature of your room.

Meanwhile, line another baking sheet with paper towels. Heat the oil in a deep-fryer or in a large heavy-bottomed pot over the stove to 375°F (190°C). The temperature of the oil is extremely important, as this determines if the donuts fry to the right coloring and also cook through on the inside.

## Donut Glaze

*4 cups (480 g) powdered sugar*

*1 tbsp (8 g) cornstarch*

*½ cup (120 ml) whole milk*

*½ tsp vanilla extract*

*Pinch of fine sea salt*

Working in batches, place 3 to 4 donuts, risen side down, in the hot oil and cook them for about 2 minutes on each side, or until the donut is a medium golden brown and not doughy in the middle.

Place the cooked donuts on the paper towel–lined baking sheet, and allow them to cool slightly. Return the pot of oil to temperature before frying the next batch.

Next, make the Donut Glaze. In a medium bowl, whisk together the powdered sugar, cornstarch, milk, vanilla, and salt. Dip the hot donuts into the glaze with a fork, letting most of the glaze drip off the donuts back into the bowl, then transfer them to a serving plate. Serve warm.

 TIP: It is nice to have a candy thermometer on hand for making donuts, especially if you are using a heavy-bottomed pot to heat the oil.

# PRAIRIE SANDWICHES, SALADS, AND HEARTY SOUPS

Do you ever wonder about the origins of food, or rather how the habits that we carry into our everyday cooking lean toward what our ancestors might have done years and years ago? For me, I tend to let my mind wander through these thoughts in the early waking hours, as I pack lunch sacks for my children. When thinking about life on the prairie when the West was young, I often ponder what a typical midday meal might have been like. Did they also pack sandwiches, freshly picked berries, and carrot sticks, and perhaps a lump of cake from the previous evening's dessert? In my mind, I can see them as I see my own little ones, sitting on a grassy knoll in their school clothes with a flour-sack towel on their laps, munching on leftover ham or sipping cold soup from a cup. It fills my heart with joy when my own family can wander down under the weeping willow trees on our farm and enjoy a little midday picnic together.

In this chapter, you will find flavorful, light meal ideas for every season. There are sandwiches such as Strawberry Chicken Salad on a Croissant (page 47) and Breaded Pork Schnitzel Sandwich with German Mustard (page 48). Perhaps you will enjoy a fresh garden salad such as Roasted Zucchini, Corn, and Cherry Tomato Salad (page 64). I love a full-bodied soup in the afternoon such as Butternut Squash, Apple, and White Cheddar Soup (page 59).

Each of these incredibly flavored dishes is a meal that I typically enjoy around lunchtime. You will find that each recipe is simple to make and absolutely delicious. They make wonderful side dishes and are perfect for bringing along on your own family picnic, spent under a shady tree, watching the birds twitter about and the wildflowers bend in the breeze.

# Pesto Chicken Panini with Chipotle Mayo

While paninis may not be the first sandwich you think of when it comes to old-fashioned cooking, this style of sandwich has, surprisingly, been around since the sixteenth century, though so-named "melted cheese sandwiches" rose to popularity in the early 1900s. Cooking bread in a pan with a deliciously melted cheese and meat filling is a small meal that people have been making for hundreds of years. This particular recipe is one that I often crave! The combination of fresh basil pesto and spicy Chipotle Mayo is absolutely packed with flavor. I love the sweet, crunchy red onion, melted mozzarella cheese, and juicy, ripe garden-fresh tomato to pair alongside a flavorful roast chicken. You might even want to try using some leftover Roasted Buffalo Butterfly Chicken (page 69) for this recipe!

## SERVES 4

### Chipotle Mayo

¼ cup (60 ml) mayonnaise

1½ tsp (7.5 ml) spicy taco sauce

1½ tsp (7.5 ml) freshly squeezed lime juice

⅛ tsp smoked paprika

⅛ tsp ground cumin

Pinch of kosher salt

Pinch of ground black pepper

### Pesto Chicken Panini

1 (12-inch [30-cm]) ciabatta loaf

¼ cup (60 ml) basil pesto

1 cup (140 g) shredded roasted chicken

8 slices prosciutto

1 medium tomato, sliced

1 cup (60 g) thinly sliced red onion

8 oz (226 g) fresh mozzarella, sliced

1 cup (30 g) fresh baby spinach

For the Chipotle Mayo, in a medium bowl, whisk together the mayonnaise, taco sauce, lime juice, paprika, cumin, salt, and pepper. Cover the bowl, and refrigerate it until you are ready to use it.

For the panini, slice the ciabatta loaf in half lengthwise. Lay the bread with the filling facing up. Pull out some of the inner part of the bread on the top piece of the ciabatta to help create room for the filling.

On the bottom piece of the bread, spread the pesto. On the top piece of the bread, spread the Chipotle Mayo. Layer the chicken, prosciutto, tomato, onion, mozzarella, and spinach on the bottom piece of the bread. Close the sandwich and slice it into four pieces.

Preheat a panini press or a large skillet over medium heat. Place the sandwiches, one at a time, into the panini press and cook them for 5 to 7 minutes, until the cheese is melted and the bread is golden brown. To make the sandwiches on the stove, cook them over medium heat, cooking for 3 to 4 minutes on each side. To give them a panini feel, use a bacon or burger press to hold down the sandwich in the skillet. Serve the sandwiches hot.

# Sun-Dried Tomato and Turkey Sandwich

I love freshly roasted turkey breast. It is on my list of favorite meats, and it makes a wonderful addition to any season of cooking, even though we often think of it as an autumnal meal. I think that this sandwich is an excellent way to use leftover meat from the Butter- and Herb-Blanketed Roast Turkey (page 71) recipe, my favorite way to roast this bird! A little spicy and tangy, this sandwich has a full-bodied flavor that you will absolutely love. The addition of homemade Roasted Garlic Aioli speaks multitudes for its freshness, and I love the pairing of pepper jack cheese and sun-dried tomatoes for a slight kick. This sandwich is a beautiful marriage of flavors.

SERVES 4–6

*Roasted Garlic Aioli*
1 small head of garlic

1 tsp olive oil

½ cup (120 ml) mayonnaise

2 tsp (10 ml) freshly squeezed lemon juice

½ tsp kosher salt

½ tsp freshly cracked black pepper

*For the Sandwiches*
1 loaf sourdough focaccia

½ cup (120 ml) Dijon mustard

½ lb (226 g) thickly sliced turkey breast

6 slices salami

1 (4-oz [114 g]) jar oil-packed roasted red peppers

½ cup (120 ml) oil-packed sun-dried tomatoes, drained and chopped into chunks

8 oz (226 g) pepper jack cheese, sliced

1 cup (30 g) mixed baby arugula and spinach

First, make the Roasted Garlic Aioli. Preheat the oven to 425°F (220°C). Cut off the top quarter of the garlic to expose the cloves inside. Place the garlic in a small shell of foil, and drizzle it with the olive oil. Enclose the garlic in the foil, and place it on a baking sheet. Roast it for about 30 minutes, or until the garlic cloves are soft and easily pierced with a fork. When the roasted garlic is cool enough to handle, squeeze the softened garlic out of their skins and into a small dish. Mash the garlic with a fork. Add the mayonnaise, lemon juice, salt, and pepper, and stir until the mixture is well combined. Set it aside.

For the sandwiches, slice the focaccia loaf in half lengthwise. Spread one half of the bread with the Roasted Garlic Aioli and the other half with the mustard.

Working with the bottom half of the bread, layer on the turkey, salami, red peppers, and sun-dried tomatoes. Top that with the cheese. Sprinkle the arugula and spinach over the cheese. Add the top half of the bread, and gently press it down to enclose the filling.

Cut the bread into four to six sandwiches. Serve them immediately, or wrap the sandwiches individually in plastic wrap, and refrigerate them for 1 to 2 days.

# Strawberry Chicken Salad on a Croissant

When the days become long and warm, we tend to spend less time cooking over the stove and more time enjoying light and fresh foods from our farm. The pioneers did similarly, with the invention of chicken salad being documented in the 1840s. Then, it was a salad made of any cold meat or fowl and homemade mayonnaise, with the addition of celery. In the summer months, we typically have fresh chicken and strawberries available around the same time. These two make a surprisingly delightful pairing as a chicken salad. This light, fresh, tangy, and slightly sweet sandwich is one of my absolute favorite sandwiches. I could eat this chicken salad all summer long and never grow tired of it! I like it served on a croissant, but it also works well on a bed of fresh greens.

## SERVES 4

3 cups (420 g) chopped cooked chicken

1 cup (240 ml) mayonnaise

1 cup (166 g) chopped fresh strawberries

3 ribs celery, chopped

2 scallions, sliced

2 tbsp (4 g) finely chopped fresh dill, plus more for garnish

2 tbsp (8 g) finely chopped fresh parsley, plus more for garnish

1 tbsp (15 ml) freshly squeezed lemon juice

2 tsp (10 ml) Dijon mustard

½ tsp kosher salt

¼ tsp ground black pepper

4 large croissants, sliced in half lengthwise

In a large bowl, with a spatula, stir together the chicken, mayonnaise, strawberries, celery, scallions, dill, parsley, lemon juice, mustard, salt, and pepper. Taste the salad, and adjust the seasonings as needed.

Spread the bottom half of a croissant with one-quarter of the chicken salad. Garnish it with more dill and parsley, then close the sandwich with the top half of the croissant. Repeat with the remaining croissants.

You can store the chicken salad in an airtight container in the refrigerator for up to 4 days.

# Breaded Pork Schnitzel Sandwich with German Mustard

This sandwich goes by the name of *Schnitzelbrötchen* in Germany. Schnitzel, made by tenderizing meat until it has become thin, then breading and frying it, is a beloved dish all over the world. While the origin of schnitzel is Germany or Austria, this would have been a common dish to see on the prairies of the western United States, as immigrants made their way over from Europe. Many here in Iowa call this a breaded pork tenderloin sandwich, not truly understanding where the beloved meal came from. You will find this local delicacy just about anywhere in the state, as Iowa is the largest pork producer in the United States. I prefer it in this more old-fashioned manner, and I know that you will, too!

## SERVES 4

### Breaded Pork Schnitzel
4 pork cutlets or thin boneless pork chops

2 tsp (12 g) kosher salt, divided

2 tsp (6 g) ground black pepper, divided

1 cup (108 g) breadcrumbs

½ cup (63 g) all-purpose flour

1 tsp dried oregano

½ tsp garlic powder

½ tsp ground white pepper

3 large eggs, beaten

¼ cup (60 ml) whole milk

Oil, for frying

### For the Sandwiches
Half head of romaine lettuce

4 brioche sandwich buns

1 large heirloom tomato, sliced

1 medium cucumber, sliced

Mayonnaise

German-style or stone-ground mustard

For the schnitzel, line a plate with paper towels and set it aside.

Pat the pork cutlets dry with paper towels. Season them with 1 teaspoon of the salt and 1 teaspoon of the black pepper on all sides, and set them aside.

In a shallow pan, mix together the breadcrumbs, flour, oregano, garlic powder, white pepper, remaining 1 teaspoon of salt, and remaining 1 teaspoon of black pepper. In another shallow pan, whisk together the eggs and milk.

Coat the pork cutlets in a layer of the flour mixture, dredge them in the egg mixture, then coat them again in the flour mixture. Set the floured cutlets on a plate, cover it with plastic wrap, and refrigerate the cutlets for 30 minutes.

Heat 1 inch (2.5 cm) of oil in a skillet over medium-high heat until it reaches 375°F (190°C) on a candy thermometer. Adjust the heat as needed to maintain the temperature. Fry two pork cutlets at a time on each side for 3 to 4 minutes, or until they are golden brown and reach an internal temperature of 145°F (63°C) on an instant-read thermometer. Transfer the cutlets to the prepared plate to drain. Return the oil to cooking temperature, then fry the second batch of cutlets.

For the sandwiches, place a piece or two of lettuce on the bottom half of the buns, followed by a piece of schnitzel and slices of tomato and cucumber. Spread the top half of the bun with a bit of the mayonnaise and German mustard. Close the sandwich, and serve it warm.

# Chicken Soup with Herbed Cracker Dumplings

I never knew how wonderful soups could be until I started making them from scratch, and they are without a doubt one of my favorite go-to meals to put together for my family. My older son will often ask me if soup is my favorite food, because I make it so often! The leading star in this recipe is the Herbed Cracker Dumplings, which can be made with any buttery cracker, whether purchased from the store or made at home. They are mixed with fresh ingredients and swell as they are cooked, making a somewhat earthy and well-seasoned dumpling that is unique from any other I have tried.

## SERVES 6

### Herbed Cracker Dumplings

1 large egg

2 tbsp (30 ml) melted salted butter

6 tbsp (32 g) crushed butter crackers

1 tbsp (15 ml) whole milk

1 tsp minced fresh parsley

¼ tsp garlic powder

¼ tsp celery salt

Pinch of ground black pepper

### Creamy Chicken Soup

4 tbsp (56 g) salted butter

1 medium onion, diced

4 ribs celery, sliced

2 medium carrots, diced

3 cloves garlic, minced

½ tsp kosher salt

½ tsp ground black pepper

1 tbsp (2 g) fresh thyme leaves

1 bay leaf

12 oz (360 ml) evaporated milk

4 cups (960 ml) chicken broth

1 cup (140 g) chopped cooked chicken breast

6 scallions, chopped, for serving

First, make the dumplings. In a medium bowl, whisk the egg and butter. Add the crackers, milk, parsley, garlic powder, celery salt, and pepper, and stir until the ingredients are well combined. Refrigerate the mixture, covered, for 30 minutes.

Meanwhile, start the soup. In a large stockpot, melt the butter over medium-high heat. Add the onion, celery, and carrots and cook until they are soft, 5 to 7 minutes. Add the garlic and cook until it's fragrant, a minute or two. Add the salt, pepper, thyme, and bay leaf.

Add the evaporated milk and chicken broth, and bring the mixture to a boil. Stir in the chicken, and simmer the soup for about 20 minutes, or until it has thickened slightly.

Scoop 1-tablespoon (14-g)-sized spoonfuls of the dumpling mixture on top of the soup. Cover the pot, and simmer the soup for 10 minutes, or until the dumplings are soft, fluffy, and no longer doughy in the middle. Remove the bay leaf and serve the soup hot, topped with the scallions to garnish.

# Creamy Loaded Potato Soup

If ever we have family or friends coming to visit, I pull out my little wooden box of recipe cards with the sunflowers on them and find the recipe to make this soup. It is as if you are eating a baked potato in the form of a soup, as the base is flavored with bacon fat and heavy cream. I love the combination of potatoes, herbs, and cheeses that creates a creamy and divinely rich meal that is beloved by anyone who tastes it. This is the most-requested soup recipe in my house. If you make it, you will soon find out why!

## SERVES 6

8 slices bacon

4 large white or russet potatoes, peeled and cut into ½-inch (1.3-cm) pieces

4 tbsp (56 g) salted butter

1 medium onion, diced

2 cloves garlic, minced

2 tsp (2 g) chopped fresh parsley or ½ tsp dried

1 tsp fresh thyme leaves or ½ tsp dried thyme

⅓ cup (42 g) all-purpose flour

2 cups (480 ml) chicken broth

2 cups (480 ml) whole milk

1 cup (240 ml) heavy cream

2 tsp (12 g) kosher salt

1 tsp ground black pepper

2 cups (226 g) shredded sharp Cheddar cheese, plus more for serving

1 cup (240 ml) sour cream

Fresh chives, for serving

Line a plate with paper towels. Heat a large skillet over medium-high heat. Cook the bacon for 5 to 6 minutes, until it's crisp, then transfer the slices to the prepared plate to drain them. Reserve 2 tablespoons (30 ml) of the bacon fat, and set it aside.

In a medium pot, cover the potatoes in water, and bring the water to a boil. Reduce the heat until the water is at a rapid simmer, and cover the pot. Cook the potatoes for 10 to 15 minutes, or until they have become slightly tender. Drain the potatoes, and set them aside.

Place the reserved bacon fat in a large stockpot. Add the butter, and cook it over medium heat, until it bubbles and is nice and hot. Toss in the onion and garlic, and cook until the onion is translucent, about 5 minutes. Toss the potatoes with the onions to coat the potatoes in the hot fat. Add the parsley and thyme, then the flour, stirring it in to coat all the vegetables.

Slowly begin to pour in the broth, 1 cup (240 ml) at a time, stirring until each cup comes to a boil. The soup should begin to thicken quickly this way. Stir frequently to prevent scorching. Add the milk and heavy cream, 1 cup (240 ml) at a time, stirring until each cup comes to a boil before adding the next. With the soup nice and thick, stir in the salt and pepper. Reduce the temperature, and simmer the soup for about 10 minutes, or until it thickens. Remove the soup from the heat, and stir in the cheese and sour cream.

Crumble the reserved bacon, and stir about half of it into the soup. Serve the soup hot, topped with the remaining bacon, Cheddar, and the chives.

# Sweet Potato and Black Bean Chili

This chili might surprise you, as it is entirely plant-based! The sweet potatoes trick the mind a bit into thinking there is some meat in the dish. I love this recipe, because it does not feel like you are eating something healthy. I have shocked many a supper guest at our table when I tell them that they just enjoyed a plant-based meal. I know that you will enjoy it, too!

## SERVES 4

### Chili

1 large sweet potato, peeled and cut into ½-inch (1.3-cm) pieces

1 tbsp + ¼ tsp (6.5 g) chili powder, divided

¾ tsp kosher salt, divided

3 tbsp (45 ml) olive oil, divided

1 small onion, diced

2 cloves garlic, minced

1 red bell pepper, diced

1 poblano pepper, diced

1 jalapeño pepper, minced

½ tbsp (3 g) cumin

¼ tsp dried oregano

1 (15-oz [425-g]) can diced tomatoes

½ cup (120 ml) water

½ tbsp (4 g) yellow cornmeal

½ tsp ground black pepper

½ tbsp (7 g) packed brown sugar

½ tsp cocoa powder

1 (15-oz [425-g]) can black beans, drained and rinsed

### For Serving

Sour cream

Fresh chives

Fluffy and Sweet Corn Bread (page 140)

For the chili, preheat the oven to 400°F (200°C). Line a baking sheet with parchment paper. Spread the sweet potato evenly on the baking sheet, season the potatoes with the ¼ teaspoon of chili powder and ¼ teaspoon of salt, and drizzle them with 1 tablespoon (15 ml) of the olive oil. Toss to coat the potatoes evenly, and roast them for 30 minutes, or until they are soft and easily pierced with a fork.

Meanwhile, heat the remaining 2 tablespoons (30 ml) of the olive oil over medium-high heat until it shimmers, about 2 minutes. Add the onion and garlic, and cook until the onion is translucent, 3 to 5 minutes. Add the bell, poblano, and jalapeño peppers, and cook until the vegetables are soft, about 3 minutes. Season the vegetables with the remaining 1 tablespoon (5 g) of chili powder, the cumin, and the oregano and toss to coat.

Pour in the diced tomatoes and water, and bring the soup to a boil. Once it's boiling, add the cornmeal, remaining ½ teaspoon of salt, the pepper, brown sugar, and cocoa. Stir in the black beans. Reduce the heat to low, and simmer the chili for 25 to 30 minutes. When the sweet potatoes have finished roasting, add them to the chili, and simmer it for 5 minutes to allow the flavors to blend.

Serve the soup hot, topped with the sour cream and chives, and alongside the corn bread.

 TIP: Chili tastes better the longer it cooks over low heat. You can make this chili in a slow cooker, if you prefer to save time. Simply roast the sweet potato as directed, then transfer the potatoes to a six-quart (5.6-L) slow cooker. Stir in all the other ingredients, and cook the chili on low for 6 to 8 hours or on high for 4 to 5 hours.

# Summertime Bacon Corn Chowder

In Iowa during the late summer months, you will find fresh sweet corn for sale at little farm stands and in the beds of pickup trucks parked on the side of the road. There is nothing quite like locally grown sweet corn, fresh from the patch, on a warm evening. Each year, we spend several afternoons peeling back the husks to reveal the creamy golden kernels underneath. One of my favorite varieties of sweet corn is Honey and Cream, and it tastes just as advertised. To pair with the subtle honey flavor in the corn, this soup is blended with a splash of local wildflower honey and applewood-smoked Cheddar. It feels like the perfect meeting of seasons, the end of summer and the beginning of autumn.

### SERVES 6

8 slices bacon, chopped

4 tbsp (56 g) salted butter

1 medium yellow onion, diced

3 cloves garlic, minced

1 (8-oz [228-g]) jar oil-packed roasted red peppers, drained

4 large corncobs sweet corn, kernels sliced off

2 medium russet potatoes, cut into ½-inch (1.3-cm) pieces

1 tsp kosher salt

1 tsp ground black pepper

1 tsp smoked paprika

1 tsp dried thyme

4 cups (960 ml) chicken or vegetable broth

1 cup (240 ml) heavy cream

1 tbsp (15 ml) wildflower honey

1 cup (116 g) shredded applewood-smoked Cheddar cheese, plus more for serving

1 cup (116 g) shredded Havarti cheese, plus more for serving

Fresh chives, for serving

Line a plate with paper towels. In a large skillet, cook the bacon over medium-high heat for 4 to 5 minutes, until it's crispy. Remove the bacon, then transfer it to the prepared plate to drain. Set it aside. Reserve 2 tablespoons (30 ml) of the bacon fat.

In a large stockpot, heat the reserved bacon fat and the butter over medium heat. Cook the onion until it's softened, about 5 minutes. Add the garlic, and cook it for 1 minute, or until it's fragrant. Stir in the roasted red peppers, and heat them for 2 minutes, or until they are warm. Stir in the corn and potatoes, then the salt, pepper, paprika, and thyme.

Add the broth and bring the mixture to a boil. Cover the pot, and reduce the heat until the mixture is at a simmer; simmer it for about 20 minutes, or until the potatoes are fork-tender. Transfer two-thirds of the soup to a food processor or blender. Pulse the soup a few times, until it's almost smooth but still a bit chunky. Return the pulsed soup to the pot.

Over medium-low heat, stir in the cream, honey, Cheddar, Havarti, and two-thirds of the bacon. Simmer the soup for 4 to 5 minutes, or until it has thickened slightly.

Garnish the hot soup with the chives, the remaining one-third of the bacon, and a bit of the Cheddar and Havarti cheeses.

# Butternut Squash, Apple, and White Cheddar Soup

Do you have deep cravings for comforting recipes when the air turns chilly in the fall? Each time the wind changes in the later part of the year, I am desperate for the flavor of squash soup. I think it makes the best warm and hearty afternoon meal, especially when paired with a piece of hot, crusty sourdough bread. It took me a bit to find the perfect combination of ingredients for a squash soup that was not too savory nor too sweet. I prefer squash soup to have a bit of a sweet flavor with the slightest hint of a peppery taste. White Cheddar pairs well with both the savory and sweet notes and brings out the undertones of the squash and fresh sage.

## SERVES 6

4 tbsp (56 g) salted butter

1 medium onion, diced

2 cloves garlic, minced

1 large sweet apple, such as Honeycrisp or Jonagold, peeled, cored, and chopped into ½-inch (1.3-cm) pieces

1 tsp kosher salt, plus more, optional

1 tsp ground black pepper, plus more, optional

1 tbsp (4 g) finely chopped fresh sage

½ tsp ground cinnamon

2 tbsp (28 g) packed brown sugar

1 medium butternut squash, peeled and cubed

4 cups (960 ml) chicken or vegetable broth

1 cup (240 ml) whole milk

1 cup (116 g) shredded sharp white Cheddar cheese

In a large stockpot, melt the butter over medium-high heat. Cook the onion for 3 to 5 minutes, until it's translucent. Toss in the garlic and most of the apple; reserve some apple pieces for garnish. Cook the apple until it is softened and fragrant, about 5 minutes. Stir in the salt and pepper. Toss the apple with the sage, cinnamon, and brown sugar.

Quickly add the butternut squash before the sugar begins to caramelize, tossing it to coat it. Add the broth, and bring it to a boil. Reduce the heat until the soup is at a simmer, cover the pan, and simmer the soup for about 20 minutes, or until the squash is soft and easily pierced with a fork. Stir the soup occasionally to prevent sticking.

Remove the pot from the heat, and carefully transfer the hot soup in batches to a food processor or blender. Pulse the mixture a few times, until it is smooth. You can also use an immersion blender for a chunkier version of the soup.

Return the soup to the stovetop over medium-low heat. Stir in the milk, and season the soup with more salt and pepper, if desired. Bring the soup back up to a simmer, then remove it from the heat and stir in the Cheddar cheese. Serve the soup warm, garnished with the reserved pieces of apple.

# Rustic Beef and Pearled Barley Stew

If you ever have the urge to travel back in time to a little tavern tucked inside a sleepy westward town, then this is the recipe for you. I love recipes that can transport you to old memories or fondly remind you of books or films that you love. I created this stew out of the desire to feel as if I stepped into a rustic place, where I could hole up for a bit with my journal, enjoying the atmosphere of people chattering over hot bowls of stew and crusty hunks of bread, and hear the rain pitter-patter on the cobblestones outside. This stew is rich and perfectly flavored with red wine, the slight licorice flavor of fennel, and deliciously tender chunks of beef.

## SERVES 6

*1 lb (454 g) beef stew meat, cut into 1-inch (2.5-cm) chunks*

*2 tsp (12 g) kosher salt, divided*

*2 tsp (6 g) ground black pepper, divided*

*4 tbsp (56 g) salted butter, divided*

*2 cups (188 g) sliced brown mushrooms*

*2 medium yellow onions, diced*

*2 large carrots, peeled and diced*

*2 large leeks, sliced thinly*

*1 small bulb fennel, chopped*

*6 cloves garlic, minced*

*1 (6-oz [170-g]) can tomato paste*

*1 tbsp (15 ml) Worcestershire sauce*

*1 tbsp (2 g) fresh thyme leaves*

*2 tsp (3 g) minced fresh rosemary*

*1 cup (240 ml) dry red wine, such as Cabernet Sauvignon*

*6 cups (1.4 L) beef broth, plus more as necessary*

*¾ cup (150 g) pearled barley*

Preheat the oven to 325°F (165°C). Season the beef all over with 1 teaspoon of the salt and 1 teaspoon of the pepper.

Place a 7-quart (6.5-L) Dutch oven over medium heat, and melt 2 tablespoons (28 g) of the butter. Brown the beef chunks in the hot fat, turning the pieces so they brown all over, for about 3 minutes total. Remove the beef from the pot, and set it aside.

Melt the remaining 2 tablespoons (28 g) of butter. Add the mushrooms, and cook them for 7 to 10 minutes, until they are browned and emitting their own juices. Stir in the onions, carrots, leeks, and fennel. Cook until the vegetables are softened, 5 to 7 minutes. Add the garlic and cook until it's fragrant, 1 to 2 minutes.

Stir in the tomato paste, Worcestershire, thyme, rosemary, remaining 1 teaspoon of salt, and remaining 1 teaspoon of pepper, until the vegetables are fully coated. Return the beef to the pot and stir to combine it. Add the wine and broth, and bring the liquids to a boil. Stir in the barley. Remove the pan from the heat.

Cover the Dutch oven, and cook the stew in the oven for 2 to 2½ hours, checking the stew occasionally to add more broth, as needed, and stirring the stew to prevent sticking. More broth is needed if the liquid has evaporated too much, and the barley is undercooked. The stew is done when the barley has become soft and tender and has soaked up most of the liquid.

# Cranberry, Walnut, and Goat Cheese Salad with Sweet Cream Dressing

This is my absolute favorite fresh salad! The combination of roasted chicken breast, sweet cranberries, crunchy red onion, creamy goat cheese, and the most amazing dressing over a bed of fresh greens is sure to make you fall in love with its simplicity. The real star of this show is the Sweet Cream Dressing, a fun play on a ranch-style dressing that brings out the delightful natural sugars in the cranberries. The dressing makes an excellent dip for fresh vegetables, as well. You might imagine this sweet salad served on a spring afternoon on a rustic wooden table with a white lace tablecloth, a pitcher of freshly squeezed lemonade, and a favorite friend seated across from you to enjoy it with.

SERVES 4

### Sweet Cream Dressing
1 cup (240 ml) mayonnaise

2 tbsp + 2 tsp (40 ml) heavy cream

1½ tbsp (22 ml) white vinegar

3 tbsp (39 g) granulated sugar

¼ tsp fine sea salt

1 tsp dried dill weed

½ tsp dried oregano

½ tsp dried parsley

### For the Salad
3 cups (90 g) fresh spring greens

3 cups (110 g) chopped fresh romaine

1 cup (140 g) shredded roasted chicken breast

1 red onion, thinly sliced

½ cup (60 g) dried cranberries

4 oz (113 g) goat cheese, crumbled

1 cup (120 g) buttery garlic croutons

To make the Sweet Cream Dressing, in a medium bowl, whisk together the mayonnaise, cream, vinegar, sugar, salt, dill, oregano, and parsley until the ingredients are well combined. The dressing can be refrigerated in a container with an airtight lid, such as a Mason jar, for up to 10 days.

For the salad, toss the greens and romaine in a large salad bowl. Top the greens with the chicken, onion, dried cranberries, goat cheese, and croutons. Serve alongside the Sweet Cream Dressing.

# Roasted Zucchini, Corn, and Cherry Tomato Salad

Looking for a perfect way to enjoy the bounty that comes from the summer garden? This warm salad is a wonderful savory treat to enjoy for your lunch as a spread on toasted bread, or even as a little starter before supper. I always picture this dish being enjoyed on an old quilt in the late afternoon after a hard day's work on the farm. Filled with fresh zucchini, sweet corn, juicy cherry tomatoes, and fresh basil, it makes for a marvelous mix of summery relishes. Don't forget the Sweet Shallot Vinaigrette!

SERVES 6

### For the Salad

3 medium zucchini, quartered and cut into ¼-inch (6-mm) chunks

2 corncobs sweet corn, husked

1 tsp kosher salt, plus more for serving

½ tsp ground black pepper, plus more for serving

2 tbsp (30 ml) extra virgin olive oil

1 cup (180 g) halved cherry tomatoes

3 scallions, sliced

½ cup (20 g) chopped fresh basil

¼ cup (15 g) minced fresh parsley

1 cup (150 g) feta cheese

### Sweet Shallot Vinaigrette

⅓ cup (80 ml) extra virgin olive oil

1 shallot, chopped finely

2 tbsp (30 ml) white wine vinegar

1 tbsp (15 ml) honey

1 tsp freshly squeezed lemon juice

¼ tsp red pepper flakes

¼ tsp kosher salt

¼ tsp pepper

For the salad, preheat the oven to 425°F (220°C). On a baking sheet, spread the zucchini and corncobs. Season them all over with the salt and pepper, and drizzle them with the olive oil. Roast the vegetables for 25 to 30 minutes, or until they are softened. Let the vegetables cool to room temperature.

With a serrated knife, slice the kernels from the roasted corn. In a large bowl, mix together the corn, zucchini, tomatoes, scallions, basil, and parsley.

Next, make the Sweet Shallot Vinaigrette. In a small skillet, heat the olive oil over medium-high heat. Cook the shallot until it's soft, 3 to 5 minutes. Add the vinegar, honey, lemon juice, red pepper flakes, salt, and pepper. Transfer the mixture to a medium bowl. With an immersion blender, blend the dressing until it's smooth.

Pour the vinaigrette over the salad, add the feta cheese, and toss to evenly coat everything.

For serving, top the salad with the kosher salt and pepper.

# MAIN DISHES FROM THE HEARTLAND

During the latter part of the nineteenth century and into the twentieth century, it was customary to eat breakfast between eight and nine o'clock in the morning, a hearty dinner by noon, and a light meal for supper; though a typical supper for those with the luxury of a cook might consist of five or six courses, including soup, bread, meat and fish, vegetables, and dessert. As many people could not afford such extravagance, an evening meal might be a bit of salt pork and potatoes, or as some of the Mennonite families still enjoy where my family lives, popcorn and apples. For most families, the availability of food was dependent entirely upon what was local to them and the season in which they were living. This is something that my own family has strived to return to, looking for wholesome ingredients that are grown and raised near where we live, and ripened within our current season. While this way of cooking has become foreign to many of us who still rely on the convenience of the grocery store, I have learned that it opens up new doors to creativity in the kitchen.

In truth, many of us crave the flavors of the season without realizing it. In summer, we wish for fresh fruits and vegetables. In autumn, pumpkin, sweet spices, and warm soups beckon. In winter, we crave meaty roasts with creamy mashed potatoes and dried fruits folded into sweet batter. Cooking with limited availability expands your pairing skills in the kitchen, and you create new dishes, much like the pioneers had to do when they first lived on the prairie.

In this chapter, you will find each entree beautifully complemented with seasonal ingredients and flavors. You might enjoy making Butter- and Herb-Blanketed Roast Turkey (page 71), Orange Marmalade–Glazed Pork Tenderloin (page 80), or Pioneer Coffee-Rubbed Roast Sirloin Tip with Bone Marrow Butter (page 94) to bring a rustic feel to your next family meal. While you do not need to live on a farm to enjoy these meals inspired by days of old, my hope is to make you feel as if you stepped right into a rustic and cozy prairie kitchen, enjoying each bite while the tall grasses dance in the breeze and birds twitter on the fence.

# Roasted Buffalo Butterfly Chicken and Baby Potatoes

During the years that I have spent sharing recipes and writing about cooking, I have found that roasting a whole chicken continues to intimidate my readers. This is one of the first meals that I learned to cook, and it was both entirely terrifying and exhilarating to conquer! For the most part, many first-time cooks are more comfortable with cooking chicken pieces, such as breasts or legs. I am here to tell you that roasting a whole chicken is far from scary. In fact, it is rather simple and a wonderful meal to make for yourself and your family. I love that we can make two to three meals from one bird: the initial meal of chicken and potatoes, chicken salad or sandwiches, then as a pizza topping or a filling for pot pie.

## SERVES 6

### Buffalo Dry Rub
1 tbsp (6 g) chili powder

2 tsp (2 g) smoked paprika

2 tsp (4 g) ground cumin

2 tsp (12 g) kosher salt

1 tsp garlic salt

½ tsp ground black pepper

½ tsp ground dry mustard

¼ tsp cayenne pepper

### Butterfly Chicken
4–5 lb (1.8–2.3 kg) whole chicken, neck and giblets removed

6 tbsp (90 ml) melted salted butter, divided

1 lb (454 g) baby potatoes, halved

2 shallots, thinly sliced

3 cloves garlic, sliced

2 tbsp (30 ml) olive oil

½ tsp kosher salt

12 oz (354 ml) sweet, hard cider or beer

For the dry rub, in a small bowl, mix together the chili powder, paprika, cumin, kosher salt, garlic salt, pepper, mustard, and cayenne. Set aside the bowl.

For the chicken, preheat the oven to 425°F (220°C). Place a 12-inch (30-cm) cast-iron skillet or Dutch oven without the lid in the oven, and preheat the pan for at least 30 minutes.

Next, pat the chicken dry with paper towels. Flip the chicken onto the breast side, with the back facing up. With sharp kitchen scissors, begin to cut along either side of the spine. Fully remove the spine; you can save it for later to make broth or discard it. Once the spine is removed, cut the collarbone in half, if the chicken is not lying flat. Flip the chicken to be breast side up, and press down on the breast to spread it open; this process may crack some ribs. You can fold the tips of the wings underneath, so that they do not burn while the chicken is roasting.

Rub the chicken all over with the Buffalo Dry Rub. With your fingers, carefully separate the fine membrane between the skin of the chicken and the meat. Rub the seasoning underneath the layer of skin, all over, including the breast, back, legs, and thighs. Be careful not to rip the skin, particularly if it is more delicate. This is the secret to incredibly flavorful chicken! Brush one-third of the butter over and underneath the skin.

*(continued)*

# Roasted Buffalo Butterfly Chicken and Baby Potatoes (Continued)

Using a potholder, remove the skillet from the oven. Evenly spread the potatoes, shallots, and garlic in the pan. Drizzle the olive oil over the vegetables, and sprinkle them with the salt, tossing gently with a spatula or wooden spoon. Place the chicken on the top of the potatoes with the breast facing up and the back fully opened over the vegetables.

Roast the chicken for 20 minutes, then remove it from the oven and brush the skin with another one-third of the butter. Return the chicken to the oven, and roast it for 20 minutes. Remove the chicken, and brush it with the remaining one-third of the butter. Roast the chicken for 20 minutes. Remove the pan from the oven, and pour the cider over the vegetables in the skillet. Roast the chicken for 15 to 20 minutes, or until the internal temperature of the chicken reaches 165°F (74°C) on an instant-read thermometer inserted into the thigh, without touching bone. Tent the chicken with foil, and allow it to rest for 10 minutes before slicing it.

 TIP: The butterfly style—where the spine is removed and the chicken is splayed open and flattened—is a wonderful way to cook a chicken, especially for a beginner, as this helps the bird to cook more evenly. You can easily do this yourself, as instructed in the recipe, or you can ask your butcher to butterfly your chicken for you.

# Butter- and Herb-Blanketed Roast Turkey

I can remember serving a whole roasted turkey to my husband for the first Thanksgiving we spent together. He had always told me that the turkey was his least favorite part of the traditional family meal, because it was dry and flavorless. This became a fun challenge for me! When Thanksgiving rolled around, out came the bird with its perfectly golden, crispy skin and dripping juices. I think I may have actually seen his eyes roll into the back of his head at the deliciousness! A large roasted turkey is one of my favorite holiday meals to make, and the art of cooking one is really quite simple. A good instant-read thermometer and lots of butter make this turkey a delectable dish for any occasion, especially those autumn and winter holidays!

## SERVES 14–16

### Turkey

14–16-lb (6.3–7.3-kg) whole turkey, with neck and giblets

2 tbsp (36 g) kosher salt

4 tsp (12 g) ground black pepper

1½ cups (336 g) salted butter, softened, divided

2 tbsp (3 g) minced fresh sage

2 tbsp (8 g) minced fresh rosemary

2 tbsp (8 g) minced fresh parsley

1 small lemon, halved

1 garlic head, unpeeled and the top sliced off

1 small onion, quartered

4 sprigs fresh thyme

2 cups (480 ml) dry white wine, such as Sauvignon Blanc

For the turkey, remove and set aside the neck and giblets. Pat the turkey dry with paper towels, including inside the cavity. Allow the turkey to sit at room temperature for 30 minutes. Meanwhile, preheat the oven to 450°F (230°C).

In a small dish, combine the salt and pepper. Rub the turkey all over with the salt-and-pepper mixture, including inside the cavity and underneath the skin. To do so, carefully separate the thin membrane between the breast meat and the skin, sliding your hand underneath and rubbing the meat with the seasoning. This ensures an extremely flavorful turkey.

With a fork, cream ½ cup (112 g) of the butter together in a small bowl with the sage, rosemary, and parsley. Rub the turkey all over with the herb butter, including underneath the skin. Stuff the cavity with the lemon, garlic, onion, and thyme. Place the turkey in a roasting pan with a rack, with the bird situated on the rack. Truss the turkey by tucking the wings underneath the body and tying the legs together with some butcher's twine. Pour the wine into the bottom of the roasting pan, and place the neck and giblets in the wine.

In a small saucepan, melt the remaining 1 cup (224 g) of butter. Remove it from the heat and let it cool slightly. Cut a 20-inch (50-cm)-long piece of double-layer cheesecloth. Completely submerge the cheesecloth in the melted butter. Squeeze the cheesecloth slightly to release some of the butter, and place it on top of the turkey, covering the outside of the bird completely. With a basting brush, baste the top of the turkey with one-third of the remaining butter, making sure it is nicely saturated.

*(continued)*

# Butter- and Herb-Blanketed Roast Turkey (Continued)

*Turkey Gravy*

¼ cup (60 ml) turkey drippings

¼ cup (32 g) all-purpose flour

1–2 cups (240–480 ml) chicken or turkey broth, or water

Roast the turkey for 30 minutes, then reduce the oven temperature to 325°F (165°C). Baste the turkey with more butter and the pan drippings. Roast the turkey for about 3 hours, or until an instant-read thermometer inserted into the thigh without touching bone reaches 165°F (74°C). Every 30 minutes while the turkey is roasting, baste it with the butter and pan drippings.

Remove the roasting pan from the oven, and tent the turkey with foil for 30 minutes. After the resting period, slice the turkey and serve it.

Make gravy from the pan drippings while the turkey rests. Remove the neck and giblets from the pan and discard them. Measure out ¼ cup (60 ml) of pan drippings. Pour the drippings in a small saucepan and place it on the stovetop. Bring the drippings to a boil over medium-high heat. Whisk in the flour until the drippings become thick. Slowly pour in 1 cup (240 ml) of the broth, whisking constantly, until the mixture comes to a boil, 6 to 8 minutes. Add more broth if the gravy is too thick. Serve alongside your turkey.

# Baked Chicken in White Wine Mushroom Sauce

I love the ease and rustic feel that this meal has, and it reminds me of old-fashioned recipes in which a game bird, such as a pheasant or wild turkey, might have been used. Chickens were not generally cooked back in the day, as their breast meat was not necessarily as plump as the hybridized breeds that we eat now. If you are looking for something more rustic, you could easily use a different type of fowl for this meal, and it would taste just as wonderful! This dish comes together in about 1 hour, making it a perfect weeknight meal to share with your family. Joining sweet apple cider with white wine, mushrooms, and thyme creates a delicious flavor palette for the creamy sauce in this dish. This chicken is delightful served over mashed potatoes, but it is also quite tasty over rice or polenta.

## SERVES 4

4 small skin-on boneless chicken breasts or 2 large breasts cut into 4 pieces

⅓ cup (42 g) all-purpose flour

1 tsp garlic powder

1 tsp kosher salt, plus more, optional

1 tsp ground black pepper, plus more, optional

8 tbsp (112 g) salted butter, divided

3 cups (210 g) sliced baby bella mushrooms

1 medium onion, diced

3 cloves garlic, sliced

1 tbsp (2 g) fresh thyme leaves or 1 tsp dried thyme

Pinch of red pepper flakes

½ cup (120 ml) chicken broth

½ cup (120 ml) apple cider

¾ cup (180 ml) dry white wine, such as pinot grigio, Sauvignon Blanc, or Chardonnay

Mashed potatoes, for serving

Preheat the oven to 375°F (190°C). Pat the chicken breasts dry with paper towels, and set them aside. In a small bowl, whisk together the flour, garlic powder, salt, and pepper. Dredge the chicken breasts in the flour mixture until all the pieces are well coated.

Heat a 2-quart (2-L) Dutch oven over medium-high heat. Melt 4 tablespoons (56 g) of the butter and place the chicken in the pan, skin side down. Cook the chicken until browned, 3 to 5 minutes per side. Place the chicken on a plate, and set it aside.

Melt the remaining 4 tablespoons (56 g) of butter over medium-high heat, and stir in the mushrooms. Stirring frequently, cook until the mushrooms are browned and have emitted their own juices, 7 to 10 minutes. Add the onion, and cook it for 3 to 5 minutes, or until it's translucent. Stir in the garlic and cook it for 1 to 2 minutes, or until fragrant. Stir in the thyme, red pepper flakes, and additional salt and pepper, if desired.

With the pan over medium-high heat, slowly pour in the chicken broth, stirring as the sauce comes to a boil. Stir in the apple cider and wine. Bring the liquids to a boil, then lower the heat for a rapid simmer. Simmer until the sauce has reduced, 10 to 15 minutes. Remove the pan from the heat.

Place the chicken in the sauce, spooning some sauce over the top. Bake, uncovered, for 30 to 35 minutes, or until the chicken reaches an internal temperature of 165°F (74°C) on an instant-read thermometer. Serve over the mashed potatoes, and cover the chicken and potatoes with the wine and mushroom sauce.

# Chicken or Steak Individual Pot Pies

Savory pies have a long history, and the pot pie is one of the simpler versions of such a creamy and rich supper. If you are new to cooking, you will learn a few essential skills here, such as making a mirepoix, making a roux, and creating a sauce. Simply cook it all up in a pot, scoop it into your favorite crust, and bake it. This version, made with chicken or steak, may easily become one of your favorites! This particular recipe uses puff pastry for a crusty topping, but pie crust is another traditional option.

## SERVES 4

1 tsp olive oil

2 tbsp (28 g) butter

1 small onion, diced

2 ribs celery, chopped

2 small carrots, peeled and chopped

1 clove garlic, minced

½ cup (70 g) ½-inch (1.3-cm) pieces cooked chicken breast or round steak

1 tbsp (4 g) chopped fresh rosemary or 1 tsp dried

1 tbsp (2 g) fresh thyme leaves or 1 tsp dried thyme

½ tsp kosher salt

½ tsp ground black pepper

2 tbsp (16 g) all-purpose flour

1 cup (240 ml) whole milk

½ cup (120 ml) chicken or beef broth

½ cup (72 g) fresh or frozen sweet peas

1 portion Easy Puff Pastry (page 152) or 1 sheet frozen puff pastry, thawed

Egg wash: 1 large egg + 1 tbsp (15 ml) water

Flaky sea salt, for serving

Preheat the oven to 425°F (220°C). Place four 8-ounce (226 g) ramekins on a baking sheet and set them aside.

In a large skillet, make the mirepoix. Heat the olive oil and butter over medium heat until the butter no longer foams. Add the onion and cook until it's translucent, 3 to 5 minutes. Toss in the celery and carrots, and cook until they are softened, about 5 minutes. Add the garlic and stir for 1 to 2 minutes, or until it's fragrant. Stir in the chicken, rosemary, thyme, salt, and pepper.

Make the roux. Sprinkle in the flour, and toss to coat all the vegetables and meat with it. Slowly begin to pour in the milk, stirring constantly. It will begin to bubble and boil quickly, thickening as it does so. Add the chicken broth in the same way, continuing to stir to prevent the food from sticking, and bring the sauce to a boil. Lower the heat to a simmer, then gently stir in the peas. Cook the filling for 5 minutes, or until the sauce is nice and thick. Remove the skillet from the heat and set it aside.

On a lightly floured surface, roll out the puff pastry into a 12 x 15–inch (30 x 38–cm) rectangle. Cut the rectangle into four 5 x 5–inch (12 x 12–cm) squares. If you are using store-bought puff pastry, skip the rolling, and cut the sheet into equal-sized squares. Use any remaining puff pastry to decorate the crust.

Scoop the pot pie filling into the mini ramekins, filling them almost to the top. Cover each ramekin with a puff pastry square, tucking the edges underneath. Make a slit in the center of the pastry for air to escape during baking. In a small dish, whisk together the egg and water for the egg wash. Brush each pastry topping with a bit of the egg wash.

Bake the pot pies for 20 minutes, or until the puff pastry is golden brown. Remove the pies from the oven, and sprinkle them with the flaky sea salt. Let the pot pies sit for at least 10 minutes before serving them.

# Chèvre- and Mushroom-Stuffed Venison Loin

When living in the country, it is common to see hunters traipsing across the harvested golden cornfields with their rifles and trusty hunting dogs at their heels. As our family prefers to eat meats that we either raise ourselves or are raised locally, hunting is another way to enjoy a variety of local meats. I love this recipe as an introduction to wild game, as it can taste quite different from a farm-raised animal. This dish really brings out the unique flavor of the venison, though it can also be made with a pork tenderloin.

## SERVES 6

5 lb (2.3 kg) venison backstrap or pork tenderloin

2 tsp (12 g) kosher salt, plus more to taste

½ tsp ground black pepper, plus more to taste

1 lb (454 g) bacon, chopped

2 tbsp (28 g) salted butter

2 cups (140 g) sliced cremini mushrooms

2 shallots, diced

3 cloves garlic, minced

2 tbsp (8 g) minced fresh rosemary

½ tsp ground nutmeg

½ cup (54 g) breadcrumbs

8 oz (226 g) chèvre cheese, crumbled

2 tbsp (30 ml) extra virgin olive oil

Preheat the oven to 350°F (180°C). Pat the venison backstrap dry. Using a sharp knife, butterfly the backstrap by slicing down the center without cutting all the way through the roast, so that it lays flat and is about ¼ inch (6 mm) thick. Rub the roast all over with the salt and pepper, then gently tenderize it with a meat mallet and set it aside.

Line a plate with paper towels. In a large skillet over high heat, cook the chopped bacon for 5 to 6 minutes, or until it's almost crispy. Place the bacon on the prepared plate to drain. Reserve 2 tablespoons (30 ml) of the bacon fat, and discard the rest. Over medium-high heat, melt the butter in the skillet with the reserved bacon fat. Add the mushrooms and cook them until they are browned and emitting their own juices, 7 to 10 minutes. Add the shallots and garlic and cook until they're soft, about 5 minutes. Stir in the rosemary, nutmeg, and more salt and pepper to taste. Remove the pan from the heat, and stir in the breadcrumbs and bacon.

Place the tenderloin on a clean surface and begin filling it with the mushroom stuffing. Sprinkle the chèvre over the mushrooms. Pull the long sides of the tenderloin together to form a long cylinder around the stuffing. With pieces of butcher's twine, tie the meat together, every 4 inches (10 cm) down the length of the backstrap.

In a large skillet, heat the olive oil over high heat until it's almost smoking, 2 minutes. Place the stuffed backstrap in the skillet, and sear it on each side for 1 to 2 minutes to brown it. Place the skillet in the oven and roast the meat for about 10 minutes, or until it reaches a perfect rare at 120° to 135°F (50 to 58°C). Overcooking the venison will result in a tougher finished meat, so it is crucial to use an instant-read thermometer. Remove the roast from the oven, cover it with foil, and let it sit for 10 minutes. For serving, slice the roast into 2-inch (5-cm) medallions.

# Orange Marmalade-Glazed Pork Tenderloin

One of my favorite parts of cooking old-fashioned meals is thinking about how they may have been served long ago. In truth, many of my recipes are reflections of meals that the average family eats today, which make them more accessible for a modern cook. I always imagine a meal such as a beautifully glazed pork tenderloin being served on an extravagantly decorated spread of fine china and silverware. However, the cooking method for this meal is rather simple, giving this roast an equally rustic charm that would be appropriate for even the humblest of tables. I love to serve this sweet and citrusy roast both during the summer, when fruits are abundant, and in the winter, for a holiday meal.

## SERVES 6

*2 lb (908 g) pork tenderloin*

*2 tbsp (28 g) packed brown sugar*

*1 tsp kosher salt*

*½ tsp ground black pepper*

*¼ cup (60 ml) orange marmalade*

*1 tbsp (15 ml) Dijon mustard*

*2 tbsp (28 g) salted butter*

Pat the pork tenderloin dry with paper towels. In a small dish, combine the brown sugar, salt, and pepper. Season the tenderloin all over with the sugar rub, and let it sit at room temperature for 30 minutes.

While the pork is resting, in a small bowl, combine the orange marmalade and Dijon; set aside the bowl.

Preheat the oven to 400°F (200°C). In a large skillet over high heat, melt the butter. Sear the tenderloin all over until it's lightly browned, 3 to 4 minutes on each side. Place the skillet in the oven, and roast the pork until it reaches an internal temperature of 145°F (63°C) on an instant-read thermometer, about 15 minutes. During the last 5 minutes of roasting, baste the tenderloin all over with the orange marmalade mixture.

Remove the roast from the oven, and tent it with foil for 5 to 8 minutes. Slice it into 1-inch (2.5-cm) medallions and serve.

# Classic Meatloaf with Sweet Tomato Sauce

In years past at our little family farm, we have hosted a handful of supper club events for friends and locals. I would typically have to choose an entree that was well received by many, and I almost always chose meatloaf. You must be thinking, "Really? Meatloaf?" It is not necessarily a meal that others have fond memories of. You either despise meatloaf, or perhaps have a more neutral feeling about it, depending on how it was cooked in your family. However, I have never met a single person who left my table without saying over and over again, "That was the absolute best meatloaf I have ever had. You have officially changed my mind!" This meatloaf is incredibly juicy, packed with flavor, and leaves you wanting more. Trust me, it is incredibly good.

## SERVES 6

### Meatloaf
1 lb (454 g) ground beef

1 lb (454 g) ground pork

½ cup (80 g) minced yellow onion

4 cloves garlic, minced

2 large eggs

1 cup (108 g) breadcrumbs

½ cup (120 ml) mayonnaise

2 tbsp (30 ml) German-style or stone-ground mustard

1 tbsp (15 ml) Worcestershire sauce

1 tbsp (2 g) dried dill weed

1 tbsp (2 g) dried parsley

2 tsp (12 g) kosher salt

1 tsp ground black pepper

1 tsp dried thyme

1 tsp dried oregano

### Tomato Sauce
1 (6-oz [170-g]) can tomato paste

3 tbsp (45 ml) chicken broth

2 tbsp (28 g) packed brown sugar

1 tbsp (15 ml) Worcestershire sauce

1 tsp apple cider vinegar

½ tsp ground cinnamon

½ tsp kosher salt

½ tsp ground black pepper

¼ tsp ginger

¼ tsp ground allspice

Preheat the oven to 350°F (180°C). Grease a 9 x 5–inch (23 x 12–cm) loaf pan and set it aside.

In a large bowl, mix the beef, pork, onion, garlic, eggs, breadcrumbs, mayonnaise, mustard, Worcestershire, dill weed, parsley, salt, pepper, thyme, and oregano with a wooden spoon or your hands until the ingredients are thoroughly combined. The meatloaf should be a bit wet and somewhat sticky, but it should be able to be formed into a large ball without crumbling.

Evenly spread the meat mixture into the loaf pan. Bake the meatloaf for 50 to 60 minutes, or until the internal temperature registers 155°F (68°C). During the last 15 to 20 minutes of cooking time, spread the Tomato Sauce evenly over the meatloaf.

Make the Tomato Sauce while the meatloaf is cooking. In a small bowl, mix the tomato paste, broth, sugar, Worcestershire, vinegar, cinnamon, salt, pepper, ginger, and allspice until the ingredients are well combined.

When the meatloaf is cooked, remove the pan from the oven, and cover the meatloaf with foil. Let it rest for 15 minutes before slicing it. The meatloaf should no longer show any signs of pinkness but will emit lots of yummy juices when it's finished!

# Baked Apple Butter Pork Chops

On our farm, we raise a handful of Berkshire hogs for our family. I will always remember the first time that I butchered a whole hog and how thrilling it was to learn about the potential meat cuts that I could make. As a cook, I believe it is important to familiarize yourself with the various cuts of meat, and how they are traditionally cooked, from any animal that you may consume. From there, you can be more creative in the kitchen and introduce yourself to using all parts of the animal. Pork chops are an exceptionally fun cut to play around with, as there are several ways to style them. For instance, as the chops are cut from the loin section of the hog, they can be made bone-in or boneless, thick-cut or thin, or, with the fancy tomahawk cut, with an entire rib attached. Because this is the most tender and flavorful part of the hog, it does not need a long cooking time. Chops can be easily baked, pan-fried, or grilled in a few minutes. This recipe in particular has a lovely smoky and sweet flavor. We love pairing apple butter with our pork chops because it brings out the sweet flavor from our pork, as our hogs spend their lives munching on fallen apples from our tiny orchard.

## SERVES 4

1 lb (454 g) boneless pork chops, about 4 chops

½ cup (112 g) salted butter, softened

1 tsp kosher salt

1 tsp ground black pepper

2 tbsp (30 ml) olive oil

2 cloves garlic, minced

2 tbsp (30 ml) apple cider or juice

2 tbsp (4 g) fresh thyme leaves

4 oz (113 g) apple butter

Preheat the oven to 400°F (200°C). Pat the pork chops dry with paper towels, and let them rest at room temperature for 30 minutes.

In a small bowl, cream together the butter, salt, and pepper, using a fork. Slather the butter mixture evenly over both sides of the chops.

Heat a large skillet over medium-high heat, and warm the olive oil until it shimmers, about 2 minutes. Place the pork chops in the skillet, and cook them until they're lightly browned, about 2 minutes per side. Add the garlic, cider, and thyme around the pork chops. Spread the apple butter over the chops and place the pan in the oven.

Bake the chops for about 15 minutes, or until the internal temperature registers 145°F (63°C) in the thickest part of the meat on an instant-read thermometer. The cooking time may vary, depending on how thickly cut your pork chops are. Let the chops rest for 5 minutes before slicing and serving them.

# Honey, Peach, and Blackberry Barbecue Pork Ribs

It is rare to see a peach tree filled to the brim with ripe, juicy peaches in Iowa, but sometimes a miracle happens, and we are graced with this sweet summertime delight. When this occurs, it becomes a slightly maddened rush to pick the peaches before they overripen in the hot July sun. Around the same time of year is when the blackberries are ready to be picked, making peaches and blackberries the perfect pair for all sorts of desserts and main dishes. A combination of sweet summer fruit, honey, and brown sugar in a from-scratch barbecue sauce gives these ribs a unique flavor.

## SERVES 4

### Baby Back Ribs

3 lb (1.4 kg) rack baby back pork ribs

2 tbsp (30 ml) wildflower honey

1 tbsp (6 g) chili powder

1 tsp garlic powder

1 tsp smoked paprika

½ tsp ground nutmeg

½ tsp kosher salt

½ tsp ground black pepper

12 oz (354 ml) stout beer

### Peach Barbecue Sauce

4 tbsp (56 g) salted butter

2 cloves garlic, minced

2 ripe peaches, peeled, pitted, and chopped

1 cup (120 g) fresh blackberries

1 cup (240 ml) orange juice

½ cup (112 g) packed brown sugar

½ cup (120 ml) tomato ketchup

2 tbsp (30 ml) Worcestershire sauce

½ tsp kosher salt

Place the ribs on a cutting board. With a knife, wedge the tip underneath the membrane on the back of the ribs to loosen it and peel it away from the bone, removing it completely.

In a small bowl, combine the honey, chili powder, garlic powder, paprika, nutmeg, salt, and pepper. Rub the mixture all over the ribs. Let the ribs sit at room temperature for 30 minutes.

Place the ribs in a slow cooker, and pour the stout in the bottom. Cover the slow cooker, and cook the ribs on low for 6 to 8 hours, or until the meat is tender and falling from the bone.

While the ribs are cooking, make the barbecue sauce. Heat the butter over medium heat in a small saucepan. Cook the garlic for 1 to 2 minutes, or until it's fragrant. Stir in the peaches and blackberries, and cook the fruit until it's warmed and the blackberries begin to pop, about 5 minutes. Add the orange juice, brown sugar, ketchup, Worcestershire, and salt. Bring the mixture to a boil, then reduce the heat so the mixture is at a simmer. Simmer the sauce, stirring occasionally, for 30 to 35 minutes, or until it's thickened and the fruit is no longer in whole pieces. Pour the sauce into a bowl through a fine-mesh sieve or cheesecloth to remove the blackberry seeds. Cover the bowl and store the sauce in the refrigerator while the ribs finish cooking.

Preheat the oven to 400°F (200°C). Line a large baking sheet with parchment paper. Place the ribs on the baking sheet, and brush them all over with the barbecue sauce. Roast the ribs for 10 to 15 minutes, or until the sauce has thickened over the ribs. Serve the ribs with any leftover barbecue sauce.

# Amish Beef and Noodles

I love a good comfort meal, and this particular dish is perfect for a warm and cozy weekend at home. This is a meal that my ancestors, living in a small Amish community, grew up eating. But I was not introduced to this dish until I was a teenager on a visit to the area where I live now. Beef and noodles is a meal that is often associated with the Midwest region of the United States, and it is typically made in a slow cooker. I like to make mine in the oven, with a homemade beef broth, flavored from a fresh beef chuck roast and vegetables. While I highly suggest using an egg noodle or even my Soft and Smooth Amish Noodles (page 144), any type of wide-cut noodle will suffice for this recipe. It slightly resembles a beef stroganoff, with less heaviness and just as much incredible flavor.

## SERVES 6

3 lb (1.4 kg) beef chuck roast

2 tsp (4 g) seasoned salt

2 tbsp (30 ml) olive oil

1 head garlic, peeled

1 large onion, quartered

1 medium green bell pepper, sliced

2 large carrots, peeled and cut into 2-inch (5-cm) pieces

4 ribs celery, cut into 2-inch (5-cm) pieces

1½ cups (90 g) chopped fresh parsley, divided

2 sprigs fresh thyme

2 sprigs fresh rosemary

2 bay leaves

2 tsp (12 g) kosher salt

1 tsp ground black pepper

2 tbsp (30 ml) Worcestershire sauce

2 tbsp (36 g) roasted beef base

2 quarts (2 L) water

1 lb (454 g) egg noodles

Preheat the oven to 325°F (165°C). Pat the chuck roast dry with paper towels, and rub it all over with the seasoned salt. Let the roast sit at room temperature for 30 minutes.

In a large Dutch oven, heat the olive oil over medium-high heat until it shimmers, about 2 minutes. Sear the roast on all sides until browned, 3 to 4 minutes per side. Remove the pot from the heat.

To the Dutch oven, add the garlic, onion, bell pepper, carrots, celery, 1 cup (60 g) of the parsley, thyme, rosemary, bay leaves, salt, pepper, Worcestershire, beef base, and water. Cover the pan and bake the roast for about 3 hours, or until the meat has an internal temperature of 195°F (90°C) on an instant-read thermometer and is falling apart.

Remove the pot from the oven, and place the roast on a cutting board. With a slotted spoon, remove the vegetables and bay leaves from the broth and discard them. Shred the meat, using two forks, and return it to the broth. Stir in the noodles. Cover the pot and return it to the oven. Cook the beef and noodles for 1 hour, 30 minutes, stirring occasionally, or until the noodles have soaked up all the broth.

Toss the remaining fresh parsley over the beef and noodles, and serve the dish warm.

# German-Spiced Beef Pot Roast with Gold Potatoes and Rainbow Carrots

While I have never been to Germany, I love learning about the recipes from across the pond that inspired the foods served here in the heart of the United States. This recipe is the perfect supper to welcome the first chilly autumn evening.

SERVES 6

*Pot Roast*
3 lb (1.4 kg) beef chuck roast

2 tbsp (28 g) salted butter

1 large yellow onion, cut into chunks

3 large rainbow carrots, peeled and cut into 3-inch (8-cm) chunks

3 medium gold potatoes, cut into 3-inch (8-cm) chunks

4 sprigs fresh thyme

4 sprigs fresh rosemary

2 bay leaves

4 tbsp (60 ml) whole-grain mustard

1 (6-oz [170-g]) can tomato paste

12 oz (354 ml) brown ale

1 cup (240 ml) beef broth

*Spiced Beef Rub*
¼ cup (56 g) packed brown sugar

2 tbsp (16 g) garlic powder

2 tbsp (14 g) onion powder

1 tbsp (18 g) kosher salt

2 tsp (4 g) dried oregano

2 tsp (4 g) dried thyme

1 tsp ground cinnamon

1 tsp ground ginger

1 tsp ground black pepper

¼ tsp ground nutmeg

For the roast, pat the chuck roast dry with paper towels and let it rest at room temperature for 30 minutes.

Make the Spiced Beef Rub while the roast rests. In a small bowl, mix together the brown sugar, garlic powder, onion powder, salt, oregano, thyme, cinnamon, ginger, pepper, and nutmeg until the ingredients are well combined. After the roast has rested, rub the spice mixture all over the meat.

In a large skillet, melt the butter over high heat. Sear the roast on all sides until browned, 4 to 5 minutes per side. Remove the pan from the heat.

Place the onion, carrots, potatoes, thyme, rosemary, bay leaves, mustard, tomato paste, ale, and broth in a slow cooker. Stir to coat all the ingredients well. Place the roast on the vegetables, cover the cooker, and cook on low for 6 to 8 hours or high for 5 to 6 hours, until the roast pulls apart easily with a fork. Serve the meat warm, surrounded by the onions, potatoes, and carrots.

# Old-Fashioned Beef and Biscuit Rolls

This is a rather unique meal and one that I have yet to come across as a typical supper choice among friends. Beef and biscuit rolls came about as an accident in my kitchen one night, while I was figuring out what I could make in a short amount of time. I needed something that would be both filling and easily enjoyed by my young children, who tend to like anything made from bread and cheese. In its most basic sense, this is a stuffed biscuit, sliced like a cinnamon roll, and filled with a mouthwatering, savory beef-and-cheese filling. This also tastes lovely with the White-Peppered Pork Sausage Gravy (page 21).

## SERVES 6

6 tbsp (84 g) salted butter, divided

1 lb (454 g) ground beef

1 medium onion, diced

1 medium green bell pepper, diced

3 cloves garlic, minced

¼ cup (15 g) minced fresh parsley

1 tsp smoked paprika

1 tsp kosher salt

½ tsp ground black pepper

½ tsp ground mustard

¼ tsp ground nutmeg

2 tbsp (16 g) all-purpose flour

½ cup (120 ml) whole milk

½ cup (56 g) shredded mozzarella

1 recipe Big Buttermilk Biscuits dough (page 143)

Flaky sea salt, for serving

Preheat the oven to 400°F (200°C). Lightly grease a 9 x 13–inch (23 x 33–cm) baking dish and set it aside.

In a large skillet, heat 4 tablespoons (56 g) of the butter over medium-high heat. Cook the beef for 5 to 6 minutes, until it's browned, crumbling it as you stir. Add the onion, green pepper, and garlic. Cook until the vegetables are softened, 5 to 7 minutes. Toss in the parsley and cook until it's wilted, about 1 minute. Add the paprika, salt, pepper, mustard, and nutmeg. Sprinkle the flour over the mixture, and toss to coat the ingredients evenly with the flour. Slowly incorporate the milk, stirring continuously, until the sauce thickens, 4 to 6 minutes. Remove the skillet from the heat, and stir in the mozzarella. Cool the mixture to room temperature.

While the filling is cooling, make the biscuit dough according to the directions on page 143. Refrigerate the dough for 25 minutes, so that the warm filling does not melt the butter in the dough when you fill and roll it.

On a lightly floured work surface, roll the biscuit dough out to a 12 x 14–inch (30 x 36–cm) rectangle. In a small saucepan, melt the remaining 2 tablespoons (28 g) of butter. Brush the biscuit dough with the butter. Spread the filling over the biscuit dough, leaving about ½ inch (1.3 cm) border all the way around.

Starting on one side of the long edge of the dough, begin rolling it toward you until the entire filling is enclosed in a biscuit log. Slice the log into 1-inch (2.5-cm)-thick pieces. Place the pieces, with the filling facing up, in the prepared baking dish. Bake the biscuits for 20 to 25 minutes, or until the biscuit is golden brown. To test the rolls for doneness, use a paring knife to gently pull apart the innermost roll and look for any dough that looks raw.

Serve the biscuits hot, topped with the flaky sea salt.

# Pioneer Coffee-Rubbed Roast Sirloin Tip with Bone Marrow Butter

A wonderful recipe is meant to be shared. I made this recipe in the middle of winter a few years ago while testing out different cuts of beef from the cow we had butchered in the spring. I had never had sirloin tip before, so it was a learning curve for me to figure out how to correctly cook this cut of meat, which is one of the more tender beef roasts that you can purchase. I loved the recipe so much that I shared it with my grandmother, who made it for friends, and they made it and shared it with their friends. This is the old-fashioned way a recipe is passed along and how a recipe becomes your grandma's famous and sentimental beef roast from who-knows-where. This roast is perfect for a fancy evening with friends or to grace your Christmas supper table. With the rich coffee and chocolate flavors mixed with the spiciness of the chili powder and cinnamon, it brings about a truly unique flavor palette that reminds me of snowy evenings spent chatting over candlelight.

## SERVES 6

### Bone Marrow Butter

6 beef marrow bones, halved lengthwise

1 tbsp (18 g) roasted garlic, from garlic roasted with the meat

½ cup (112 g) salted butter, softened

½ tsp fine sea salt

½ tsp freshly cracked black pepper

### Beef Tip Roast

3–4 lb (1.4–1.8 kg) sirloin tip roast

¼ cup (20 g) finely ground coffee

¼ cup (56 g) packed brown sugar

2 tbsp (6 g) smoked paprika

1 tbsp (6 g) chili powder

1 tsp ground cinnamon

1 tsp Dutch-process cocoa powder

1 tsp kosher salt

1 tsp ground black pepper

½ tsp garlic powder

First, begin making the bone marrow butter. Preheat the oven to 425°F (220°C). Line a baking sheet with parchment paper. Place the marrow bones with the marrow side up on the baking sheet. Roast the bones for 20 minutes, or until the marrow is soft. Scrape out the marrow into a small bowl. Cover and refrigerate the marrow until you're ready to use it.

For the roast, pat the meat dry with paper towels. In a small bowl, combine the coffee, brown sugar, paprika, chili powder, cinnamon, cocoa, salt, pepper, and garlic powder. Rub this mixture all over the sirloin tip, and let the meat rest at room temperature for 30 minutes. Fifteen minutes before the end of the resting time, preheat the oven to 400°F (200°C).

1 large onion, roughly chopped

2 large carrots, roughly chopped

6 cloves garlic, unpeeled

Fresh parsley sprigs, for serving

Place the onion, carrots, and garlic in a large Dutch oven. Place the roast on top of the vegetables. Bake the roast for 30 minutes. Lower the oven temperature to 325°F (165°C), and roast the meat for 1 hour to 1 hour and 25 minutes, or, for medium rare, until the internal temperature registers 130°F to 135°F (54 to 58°C) on an instant-read thermometer. Tent the roast with foil and let it rest for 15 to 20 minutes before slicing it.

While the meat is resting, remove the scraped bone marrow from the refrigerator. Retrieve the garlic cloves from the Dutch oven, then squeeze the garlic from their skins into the bowl with the bone marrow. With a spatula or handheld electric mixer, whip together the marrow, roasted garlic, butter, salt, and pepper. Form the mixture into a small log, wrap it with plastic wrap, and refrigerate until you are ready to use it.

Slice the meat and the log of marrow butter. For serving, top slices of the meat with a slice of the butter and the parsley, and plate alongside the carrots and onions.

# Summertime Beer-Battered Walleye

In the Iowa Heartland, walleye is generally served during the peak summer months, when fresh fish can be found in most lakes, rivers, and ponds around the countryside. We try our best to eat locally caught freshwater fish, rather than those you would find on the coasts. This ensures that the fish is fresh and at its best for eating. In the late summer, we love to eat fried catfish and walleye. It is, in many ways, an Iowa staple, along with bluegill and crappie. This recipe makes for a wonderful summertime fry, with its thick, crispy batter and incredibly seasoned, flaky walleye. It is wonderful paired with all the fixings, including freshly made cabbage coleslaw, roasted corn, Cheddar biscuits, cucumber salad, and strawberry pie.

## SERVES 4

*4 walleye filets, about 1 lb (454 g)*

*2 tsp (12 g) kosher salt, divided*

*2 tsp (6 g) ground black pepper, divided*

*1½ cups (188 g) all-purpose flour, plus more for dusting*

*½ cup (64 g) cornstarch*

*2 tsp (8 g) baking powder*

*1 tsp smoked paprika*

*1 tsp garlic powder*

*1 tsp dried oregano*

*½ tsp chili powder*

*½ tsp dried thyme*

*½ tsp ground white pepper*

*Pinch of cayenne pepper*

*12 oz (354 ml) light beer*

*Oil, for frying*

*Tartar sauce, for serving*

*Sweet Cabbage Coleslaw (page 113), for serving*

Pat the walleye filets dry with paper towels. Season them all over with 1 teaspoon of the salt and 1 teaspoon of the pepper. Lightly dust each filet in a bit of flour, and set it aside.

In a large bowl, combine the flour, cornstarch, baking powder, paprika, garlic powder, oregano, chili powder, thyme, white pepper, cayenne, the remaining 1 teaspoon salt, and the remaining 1 teaspoon black pepper. Pour in the beer, and mix the ingredients until a thick batter is formed.

Line an oven-safe plate with paper towels, and preheat the oven to Warm or 200°F (100°C).

Put oil that is at least 2 inches (5 cm) deep in a large skillet or Dutch oven. Heat the oil over medium-high heat to 375°F (190°C) on a candy thermometer, maintaining that temperature throughout the frying process. Dip the filets in the beer batter until they are fully coated; the coating will be quite thick. Fry the filets, two at a time, until golden brown, 3 to 4 minutes on each side. The fish is finished when it reaches an internal temperature of 145°F (63°C) on an instant-read thermometer.

Place the finished filets on the prepared plate to drain, putting the first two filets in the oven to keep them warm while you fry the others.

Serve the walleye hot, with the tartar sauce and coleslaw.

# Crab- and Parmesan-Stuffed Whole Catfish

I love a freshly caught catfish. My husband loves to take our sons fishing, and the big hope is that they will bring home a fine-looking catfish for me to cook up. There are many ways to cook a fish, but I absolutely love this particular dish for a fancier evening meal. This is just simple enough for the beginner cook to prepare and has the ability to impress your guests, as it looks like something you slaved over all afternoon!

## SERVES 4

*4 catfish filets, about 1 lb (454 g)*

*1 tsp kosher salt, divided*

*½ tsp ground black pepper, divided*

*2 tbsp (30 ml) olive oil, divided*

*2 tbsp (28 g) salted butter*

*1 small yellow onion, diced*

*1 medium green bell pepper, diced*

*2 cloves garlic, minced*

*4 oz (113 g) lump crabmeat*

*2 tsp (4 g) Italian seasoning*

*1 tbsp (15 ml) balsamic vinegar*

*¼ cup (60 ml) dry white wine, such as Sauvignon Blanc*

*¼ cup (28 g) breadcrumbs*

*½ cup (50 g) grated Parmesan cheese, divided*

*1 small lemon, cut into 4 wedges, for serving*

Preheat the oven to 350°F (180°C). Line a baking sheet with parchment paper and set it aside. Pat the catfish filets dry with paper towels. Season the filets all over with ½ teaspoon of the salt and ¼ teaspoon of the pepper. Set aside the filets.

In a large skillet, heat 1 tablespoon (15 ml) of the olive oil and the butter over medium heat. Cook the onion and bell pepper until soft, about 5 minutes. Stir in the garlic, and cook until it's fragrant, 1 to 2 minutes. Add the crabmeat, and stir until it's coated in the fat. Sprinkle in the Italian seasoning, the remaining ½ teaspoon of salt, and the remaining ¼ teaspoon of pepper.

Pour in the balsamic vinegar and wine. Stir and cook the mixture for 5 minutes, until the liquid has almost reduced by half. Stir in the breadcrumbs and cook them for 4 to 6 minutes, or until lightly toasted. Remove the pan from the heat, and stir in half of the Parmesan. Set the stuffing aside to cool slightly.

Meanwhile, butterfly the catfish filets. Starting at one end on the longest side of the filet, run a knife along the entire side, making a long cut across the edge of the entire filet. Carefully slice through the meat, as if slicing a bun in half, and stopping before you reach the opposite side. Leaving the other side of the filet attached, carefully open it up, giving yourself a top half and a bottom half to stuff.

Place the filets on the prepared baking sheet, spread ¼ cup (28 g) of crab stuffing inside each filet, and close them. Secure the closure with toothpicks, if desired. Drizzle the remaining 1 tablespoon (15 ml) of olive oil evenly over the filets, and sprinkle the remaining Parmesan evenly over them.

Bake the fish for 20 minutes, or until the thickest part of the fish registers 145°F (63°C) on an instant-read thermometer. A fully cooked fish will no longer look transparent and will flake when twisted with a fork. Serve the fish hot, topped with a lemon wedge to squeeze over it.

# Spinach, Mushroom, and Feta Quiche

While many associate a deliciously creamy and fluffy quiche with French cuisine, the origins of quiche lie with the Germans. It comes from the German word *kuchen*, which translates to "cake." This particular quiche makes a wonderful meal to cook ahead of time, and is perfect if you'd like to skip the meat for a change!

## MAKES 1 (10-INCH [25-CM]) PIE

Single Crisp and Flaky Pie Crust (page 151)

5 large eggs

½ cup (120 ml) heavy cream

2 tsp (12 g) kosher salt, divided, plus more, optional

½ tsp pepper, divided, plus more, optional

2 tbsp (28 g) salted butter

1 cup (70 g) thinly sliced cremini mushrooms

1 medium yellow onion, diced

2 cups (60 g) shredded fresh baby spinach

3 cloves garlic, minced

2 tsp (3 g) fresh thyme leaves or 1 tsp dried thyme

6 oz (170 g) feta cheese

8 oz (226 g) shredded mild Cheddar cheese, divided

Egg wash: 1 large egg + 1 tbsp (15 ml) water

Prepare your pie crust according to the directions on page 151. Cover the dough in plastic wrap, and refrigerate until ready to use. Preheat the oven to 375°F (190°C). In a small bowl, whisk the eggs until slightly foamy. Add the cream, and whisk to combine it. Season the egg mixture with 1 teaspoon of the salt and half of the pepper and set it aside.

In a large skillet, melt the butter over medium-high heat. Add the mushrooms and cook them until they are browned and they emit their own juices, 7 to 10 minutes. Toss in the onion, and cook until translucent, about 5 minutes. Add the spinach to the skillet and cook until it's wilted, a minute or two. Add the garlic, and cook for a minute, or until it's fragrant. Stir in the thyme, the remaining 1 teaspoon of salt and the remaining pepper. Remove the skillet from the heat, and stir in the feta and 6 ounces (170 g) of the Cheddar.

Remove the pie dough from the refrigerator, and place it on a lightly floured surface. Roll out the dough into a circle about 12 inches (30 cm) in diameter, making sure to roll all the way to the edges. If the dough cracks while rolling, allow it to sit at room temperature for 10 minutes, then try rolling it again. Place the dough in a 10 x 2–inch (25 x 5–cm) pie plate. Leave a 1-inch (2.5-cm) lip of crust around the edge of the pie plate, fold it under, and crimp the edges. Pierce the bottom of the crust all over with the tines of a fork. In a small dish, whisk together the egg and water for the egg wash. Brush the egg wash all over the crust, including the edges and bottom. Pour the vegetable filling from the skillet into the crust. Pour the egg-and-cream mixture over the filling and spread it until it covers all the vegetables. Season the quiche with more salt and pepper, if desired.

Bake the quiche for 15 minutes. Remove the pie from the oven, and sprinkle it with the remaining Cheddar. Bake the quiche for 40 to 45 minutes, or until the center is no longer jiggly. Place foil around the edges for the last 20 minutes of baking and then allow the quiche to stand at room temperature for at least 20 minutes before slicing it.

# HOME-COOKED
# STARTERS AND SIDES

To create a colorful plate, many main dishes can be accompanied by a vegetable and a delicious starchy side. For me, I tend to love side dishes more than the main event, as they are often the parts filled with gooey cheeses, flavorful homegrown vegetables, and perhaps even something a bit naughty, such as a fried treat or sweet fruit. In our community of farmers, throughout the seasons we enjoy potluck gatherings with a variety of accompaniments alongside a savory meat or rich soup.

In spring, we love the return of fresh vegetables from the garden, such as an earthy green salad or roasted broccoli, and we use the remainder of the previous year's preserves baked with pastry. In summer, the table is filled with the kings and queens of the season, such as cucumbers, zucchini, heirloom tomatoes, and sweet corn. When autumn arrives, we delve into soft and sweet winter squash and fried apples, and, in the middle of winter, we enjoy those foods that we harvested and preserved, such as hearty potatoes and crisp rainbow carrots. With starters, salads, and side dishes, I like to execute my creativity and to introduce exciting flavors to our family meals.

In this chapter, there are some fun recipes, such as Miniature Pommes Anna (page 105), Campfire Boston Baked Beans (page 114), Country Slow Cooker Cinnamon Apples (page 118), and my famous Green Bean Casserole with French Fried Scallions (page 120). These are some of our absolute favorite sides to decorate any meal and to turn it into something filling and delicious.

# Miniature Pommes Anna

This recipe is a play on the classic pommes Anna or potatoes Anna, a French way of layering potatoes that are cooked in a rather large amount of butter and smashed. According to Iowa history, the first European explorers to discover the lush, fertile state were Frenchmen in 1673. It would not be surprising to find varying versions of this dish among settlers, as it was invented in the mid- to late nineteenth century. Typically, this delicate potato dish is cooked in a quiche pan at a high temperature until the potatoes are crispy, after which the dish is sliced like a piece of pie or cake. This version is a yummy, little melt-in-your-mouth treat, especially when baked in a miniature individual portion! This makes it simple, as well as a delightful presentation for guests.

## SERVES 6

*2 lb (908 g) baby gold potatoes*

*½ cup (120 ml) melted salted butter*

*2 tbsp (36 g) kosher salt*

*2 tsp (6 g) ground black pepper*

*2 tbsp (4 g) fresh thyme leaves, plus more for serving*

*1 cup (100 g) grated Parmesan cheese*

*Flaky sea salt, for serving*

Preheat the oven to 400°F (200°C). Grease a standard 12-cup muffin tin. Set it aside.

Prepare a bowl of ice water. Use a mandoline to cut the potatoes into ⅛-inch (4-mm) pieces, and drop the slices in the ice water as you cut them to prevent them from browning or over softening.

In a large bowl, stir together the butter, salt, pepper, thyme, and Parmesan. Drain the potatoes, pat them dry, and toss them in the butter mixture until they are evenly coated.

Stack the potatoes in the muffin-tin cups, filling them to the top of the tin. Spray a piece of foil with cooking spray, and use it to cover the entire muffin tin. Roast the potatoes for 30 minutes. Remove the foil, and cook the potatoes for 30 minutes, or until they are fork-tender, golden, and crispy. Top the potatoes with the sea salt and thyme leaves.

# Mincemeat Hand Pies

Have you ever had true mincemeat? I love to make it for the holidays. As a traditional English holiday dessert, mincemeat pies make lovely little starters for a special meal or a treat on Christmas Eve. In fact, they are even believed to bring luck and good fortune on the eve of the new year! Traditionally, mincemeat is made with chopped, boiled beef or lamb, brandy, and suet. As those ingredients can be a bit more difficult to come by, I prefer to make this simpler version. The flavor of tallow or lard really brings an old-fashioned feeling to this recipe. It's entirely sweet and tricks you a bit into forgetting that the inside filling contains ground beef!

## SERVES 6

*Double Crisp and Flaky Pie Crust (page 151)*

*½ lb (226 g) ground beef*

*¼ cup (58 g) tallow or lard*

*1 medium apple, peeled, cored, and chopped into ½-inch (1.3-cm) pieces*

*½ cup (120 ml) apple cider or brandy*

*2 tsp (10 g) packed brown sugar*

*1 tsp ground cinnamon*

*½ tsp ground black pepper*

*¼ tsp ground nutmeg*

*Pinch of kosher salt*

*¼ cup (40 g) chopped raisins*

*¼ cup (40 g) chopped golden raisins*

*⅛ cup (25 g) chopped dried candied orange pieces*

*Egg wash: 1 large egg + 1 tbsp (15 ml) water*

Preheat the oven to 400°F (200°C). Line a baking sheet with parchment paper and set it aside. Make the pie crust and refrigerate it, wrapped in plastic wrap, until you are ready to use it.

In a large skillet over medium-high heat, cook the beef for 7 to 10 minutes, or until it's browned, crumbling it as you stir. Remove the pan from the heat, and drain any excess fat.

In a large bowl, combine the tallow, apple, cider, brown sugar, cinnamon, pepper, nutmeg, salt, both types of raisins, and candied orange. Thoroughly mix the ingredients. Add the beef, and mix until it's well combined with the fruit mixture.

Divide the pie dough into two equal pieces. Roll out one piece of the pie dough to a 12-inch (30-cm) round. With a 2-inch (5-cm) round biscuit or cookie cutter, begin cutting out rounds.

For the egg wash, whisk together the egg and water. Beginning with one round of the pie dough, brush it with egg wash. Place 1 to 2 tablespoons of mincemeat filling in the center. Place a second piece of cut pie dough on top, and press all around the edges with the tines of a fork. With a sharp knife, make a small slit in the top center of the dough. Brush the top with the egg wash, and place the pie on the prepared baking sheet. Repeat until the pie dough and mincemeat filling is used up. If your pie dough is sticking to your fingers or the counter, it is becoming too soft, and if the butter visually begins to melt, it's too warm. In either case, refrigerate the dough for 20 minutes before continuing to build the pies.

Bake the pies for 35 to 40 minutes, or until the pie crust is golden brown and the filling is bubbly inside.

# Old-Fashioned German Potato Pancakes

Whenever I make these potato pancakes, my dad tells me that it reminds him of sitting at his grandmother's kitchen table for breakfast when he was a little boy. My great-grandparents were German immigrants who moved to the United States during the Second World War. With them, they brought the traditional foods of their German and Polish heritage. It has been my quest to uncover a lot of the recipes that my father enjoyed as a child, as they were never passed down to us. I was absolutely elated to learn that these potato pancakes were almost identical to the ones that he ate as a boy! I hope that this recipe brings back kindred memories or begins new ones for you as well.

## SERVES 6

*3 cups (630 g) leftover mashed potatoes*

*1 cup (114 g) shredded sharp Cheddar cheese*

*¼ cup (40 g) finely diced onion*

*¼ cup (15 g) minced fresh parsley, plus more for serving*

*½ cup (64 g) all-purpose flour, plus more as needed*

*½ tsp garlic powder*

*½ tsp kosher salt*

*½ tsp ground black pepper*

*1 large egg*

*4 tbsp (60 ml) olive oil*

*Sour cream, for serving*

In a large bowl, combine the potatoes, Cheddar, onion, parsley, flour, garlic powder, salt, pepper, and egg. The mixture should be a bit on the dry side, and you should be able to form the mixture into a ball with your hands without it being too sticky. You may need to add more flour, depending on how moist your mashed potatoes are.

Sprinkle some flour onto a plate, and put a sheet of wax paper on the counter. Roll about ¼ cup (60 g) of the potato mixture into a ball, then dredge the ball in the flour. Place the ball on the wax paper, and press down on it with a spatula until it's ½ inch (1.3 cm) thick. Roll and flatten the remaining mixture.

Line a baking sheet with paper towels, and place a wire rack over the towels. Heat a large skillet over medium-high heat. Heat the olive oil until it shimmers, about 2 minutes. Cook the potato pancakes, four at a time, for 3 to 4 minutes per side, or until they are golden brown and hold together. Transfer the potato pancakes to the wire rack to drain as you cook each batch. Serve the pancakes hot, with the sour cream and parsley.

# Creamy Baked Macaroni and Cheese with Smoked Gouda

Is there anything better than a bowl filled to the brim with warm, creamy macaroni and cheese? My kids absolutely love this dish, as most children do, and it is one that I love, too, because it comes together so quickly. I started learning to cook from scratch for this reason: to feed my children excellent homemade foods! This was simply one way to incorporate a wholesome meal—not from a box—into their diets. I do not know if we will ever go back! This recipe is incredibly good as a main meal, but I like to make it at this portion size for a side dish at the supper table. I highly recommend using a smoked cheese, if you can, as it truly brings something extra to an otherwise simple recipe.

## SERVES 4–6

1½ cups (226 g) elbow macaroni

3 tbsp (42 g) salted butter, divided

1 tsp kosher salt, divided

½ cup (58 g) shredded sharp Cheddar cheese

½ cup (58 g) shredded smoked Gouda cheese

¼ cup (34 g) shredded white Cheddar cheese

1 tbsp (8 g) all-purpose flour

1½ cups (360 ml) whole milk

1 tsp smoked paprika

1 tsp garlic powder

½ tsp ground black pepper

Preheat the oven to 375°F (190°C). Lightly grease a 9 x 9–inch (23 x 23–cm) baking dish and set it aside.

In a medium saucepan, cook the macaroni according to the package directions for al dente. Drain the elbows, then toss them with 1 tablespoon (14 g) of the butter and ½ teaspoon of the salt. Set aside the elbows.

In a medium bowl, stir together the sharp Cheddar, Gouda, and white Cheddar. Measure ½ cup (58 g) of the mixed cheeses, and set it aside.

For the sauce, in a medium saucepan, melt the remaining 2 tablespoons (28 g) butter over medium heat. Whisk in the flour and cook it for 2 minutes, until the flour is lightly browned, and it begins to give off a nutty aroma. Pour in the milk, continuing to whisk, until it comes to a boil and thickens slightly. Stir in the paprika, garlic powder, pepper, and remaining ½ teaspoon of salt. The sauce should be a bit thin; it will thicken while baking.

Remove the sauce from the heat, and stir in the bowl of mixed cheeses.

Spread the cooked macaroni in the prepared dish. Pour the sauce over it, then stir to fully cover all the noodles. Sprinkle the reserved ½ cup (58 g) of mixed cheeses over the macaroni. Bake the mac and cheese, uncovered, for 15 to 20 minutes, or until the sauce is thickened and the cheese on top is golden.

# Sweet Cabbage Coleslaw

Coleslaw has not always been a side dish. In fact, it was a main meal eaten as far back as Ancient Rome, and it used the same mixture of ingredients that we use today: cabbage, eggs, vinegar, and seasonings. The Dutch brought their own cabbage salad, called *koosla*, with them to the American colonies. As mayonnaise has only been around for about three centuries, this makes the modern American version still a bit fresh. Today, coleslaw is eaten as an accompaniment to barbecue or fried chicken. I have eaten lots of homemade coleslaws over the years, and I love the dressing for this recipe. It's undeniably sweet and crunchy, with a hint of sour flavoring from the buttermilk. Try this recipe at your next summer cookout!

## SERVES 4

*1 small head green cabbage, chopped finely*

*1 small head purple cabbage, chopped finely*

*1 cup (110 g) shredded carrots*

*1 cup (110 g) shredded kohlrabi*

*1 cup (200 g) granulated sugar*

*1 tsp kosher salt, plus more for serving*

*1 tsp freshly cracked black pepper, plus more for serving*

*1 tsp celery seed*

*¼ tsp ground nutmeg*

*1 cup (240 ml) mayonnaise*

*1 cup (240 ml) buttermilk*

Mix the green cabbage, purple cabbage, carrot, kohlrabi, sugar, salt, pepper, celery seed, nutmeg, mayonnaise, and buttermilk in a large bowl until the ingredients are well combined. Cover the bowl with plastic wrap, and refrigerate the coleslaw for at least 6 hours or overnight. Serve the slaw cold with a bit of salt and pepper.

# Campfire Boston Baked Beans

A summer barbecue is not complete without a side of baked beans! I grew up always eating sweet, brown sugar–baked beans in the summer, usually from a can, but I have learned to love them in the middle of winter, too. This recipe tastes just like they came off the camp stove! Sweet, syrupy, and warm, they pair wonderfully with a big bowl of mashed potatoes or a slice of roast turkey. It is fairly easy to make homemade baked beans; all it takes is some time. If you would like to move away from store-bought foods, add this recipe to your list for something entirely made from scratch!

## SERVES 6

*3 cups (549 g) dried navy beans*

*8 slices bacon, cut into 1-inch (2.5-cm) pieces*

*2 cups (480 ml) chicken broth, plus more as needed*

*1 (15-oz [425-g]) can diced tomatoes*

*2 large onions, diced*

*1 cup (240 ml) ketchup*

*1 cup (240 ml) blackstrap molasses*

*½ cup (112 g) packed brown sugar*

*1 tbsp (6 g) ground mustard*

*1 tsp kosher salt*

*½ tsp ground black pepper*

Place the beans in a 7-quart (6.5-L) Dutch oven, and cover them with 2 quarts (2 L) of water. Bring the water to a boil over medium-high heat. Reduce the heat slightly, and cook the beans at a gently rolling boil for 5 minutes. Remove the pot from the heat, cover it, and let it stand for 1 hour.

Drain the beans. Return them to the pot with 3 quarts (3 L) of water. Bring the pot to a boil, reduce the heat to a simmer, cover the pot, and cook the beans for 45 to 50 minutes, or until they are tender when pierced with the tip of a paring knife. Drain the beans and set them aside.

Preheat the oven to 325°F (165°C). Line a plate with paper towels. In a large skillet, cook the bacon over medium heat for 4 minutes, until the fat is rendered but it's not fully crisped. Drain the bacon on the prepared plate.

In a 6-quart (5.6-L) Dutch oven, combine the beans, broth, tomatoes, onions, ketchup, molasses, brown sugar, mustard, salt, pepper, and the cooked bacon. Cover the pot and bake the beans for 1 hour, checking the sauce level occasionally. If the sauce has reduced and there is little liquid left in the pot, add up to 1 cup (240 ml) more of chicken broth. The beans will still be somewhat firm at this stage of cooking. Uncover the pot and cook the beans for 1 to 1½ hours, stirring occasionally, or until the sauce is thick and syrupy and the beans are soft.

# Browned Butter Three-Cheese Mashed Potatoes

These mashed potatoes are a frequent request when I am invited to a potluck or gathering. In my experience, a truly good mashed potato recipe is difficult to find. After years of simply adding some butter and sour cream to my potatoes, I discovered the trick truly does come from adding in just the right amount of liquid. These potatoes achieve the perfect consistency with chicken broth, milk, and heavy cream. The blend of cheeses brings about a creamy texture full of divine savory flavors.

## SERVES 6

5 lb (2.3 kg) unpeeled gold potatoes, cubed

1 cup (240 ml) chicken broth

1½ cups (360 ml) whole milk

½ cup (120 ml) heavy cream

½ cup (112 g) salted butter

4 cloves garlic, minced

1 cup (113 g) shredded sharp Cheddar cheese

1 cup (113 g) shredded Emmental or Swiss cheese

½ cup (50 g) grated Parmigiano-Reggiano cheese

2 tsp (12 g) kosher salt, plus more to taste

1 tsp ground black pepper, plus more to taste

Chopped fresh chives, for serving

Place the potatoes in a large stockpot, and cover them completely with water. Bring the water to a boil, cover the pan, reduce the heat, and maintain a gentle boil. Cook the potatoes for about 20 minutes, or until they are fork-tender. Drain the potatoes and return them to the stockpot. Stir in the chicken broth, milk, and heavy cream. Cover the pan and set it aside.

In a small saucepan, melt the butter over low heat, stirring it continually so as not to let it burn. Once the butter is melted, add the garlic. Stir and cook the mixture over medium-low heat until the butter begins to brown and has a bit of a nutty aroma, about 5 minutes.

With a handheld electric mixer or wooden spoon, whip the potatoes for 5 to 7 minutes, or until they are smooth. Add the browned butter to the potatoes, along with the Cheddar, Emmental, Parmigiano-Reggiano, salt, and pepper. Stir until the cheese has melted. Taste the potatoes, and add more salt and pepper, if desired. Serve the potatoes hot, topped with the chives.

# Country Slow Cooker Cinnamon Apples

If you have ever wanted to bring the sweet scents of autumn into your home, there is nothing sweeter than cooking up a large pot of apples. This is a side that I simply cannot eat enough of, as it tastes like warm apple pie filling! It is wonderful served with pork or fried chicken. Make these in a slow cooker for a simple side dish that is ready for your late lunch or supper. I love to use Jonagold or Braeburn apples best, but Honeycrisps are a good substitute. The aroma will truly fill up your entire house and have your family asking when they will be ready to eat!

SERVES 6

3 lb (1.4 kg) Jonagold, Braeburn, or Honeycrisp apples, peeled, cored, and cut into ½-inch (1.3-cm) wedges

2 tbsp (16 g) cornstarch

¼ cup (56 g) packed brown sugar

¼ cup (50 g) granulated sugar

2 tsp (6 g) ground cinnamon

1 tsp vanilla extract

4 tbsp (56 g) salted butter

Freshly squeezed juice of 1 lemon

Pinch of fine sea salt

In a slow cooker, gently stir to combine the apples, cornstarch, brown sugar, granulated sugar, cinnamon, vanilla, butter, lemon juice, and salt. Cover the slow cooker, and cook the mixture on high for 2 to 3 hours, or until the apples are tender and the sauce is thick.

# Green Bean Casserole with French Fried Scallions

This casserole has been a family favorite for years, and we often eat it during the winter months. Deliciously rich, creamy, comforting, and somewhat green, it makes for a perfect side dish for your next supper. I love this recipe because it is incredibly simple to make, even seemingly in comparison to the conventional version that uses canned foods. Rather than a can of soup, you will make your own roux and béchamel sauce to coat the green beans and onions. The french fried scallions are quickly fried in minutes on the stovetop, for a fresh, crispy topping. If you do not have a Dutch oven, you can simply prepare this casserole on the stove, then transfer it to a 9 x 13–inch (23 x 33–cm) casserole dish with a lid, or a foil cover, for baking.

## SERVES 6

### Green Bean Casserole

2 lb (908 g) fresh green beans, ends trimmed

2 tbsp (30 ml) olive oil

6 tbsp (84 g) salted butter

1 lb (454 g) cremini mushrooms, sliced

½ tsp kosher salt, divided, plus more to taste

½ tsp ground black pepper, divided, plus more to taste

2 tsp (1 g) fresh thyme leaves

4 tbsp (32 g) all-purpose flour

1¼ cups (300 ml) whole milk

1 cup (240 ml) heavy cream

6 cloves garlic, minced

½ cup (50 g) grated Parmesan cheese

In a large stockpot, cover the green beans with water, and bring it to a boil. Boil the beans for 3 minutes. Drain the pot, and immediately rinse the beans in cold water. Set them aside.

Preheat the oven to 375°F (190°C).

In a 2-quart (2-L) Dutch oven, heat the olive oil and butter on the stove over medium heat. Toss in the mushrooms, and sauté them until they are browned and begin to release their own juices, 7 to 10 minutes. Add ¼ teaspoon of the salt and ¼ teaspoon of the pepper. Add the thyme, and stir until it's fragrant.

Sprinkle the mushrooms with the flour, stirring constantly to prevent scorching, until the flour is lightly browned and begins to give off a nutty aroma, about 2 minutes. Slowly pour in the milk in a steady stream, stirring constantly. It will begin to thicken quickly. Stirring constantly, bring the mixture to a boil, then pour in the heavy cream in a steady stream, stirring constantly. Once the sauce has come to a boil, lower the heat to a simmer. Cook and stir the sauce for 5 to 7 minutes, or until the sauce is thick enough to coat the back of a spoon. Remove the sauce from the heat, and stir in the garlic, Parmesan, and remaining ¼ teaspoon of salt and ¼ teaspoon of pepper.

To the mushroom sauce, add the blanched green beans. Stir with a spatula or wooden spoon until everything is evenly coated. Cover the Dutch oven and bake the casserole for 40 minutes.

## French Fried Scallions

1 cup (125 g) all-purpose flour

1 tsp kosher salt

1 tsp ground black pepper

1 tsp smoked paprika

½ tsp garlic powder

1 large egg

¼ cup (60 ml) whole milk

3 scallions, sliced thinly

4 tbsp (60 ml) olive oil

Meanwhile, make the French Fried Scallions. Line two baking sheets with paper towels. In a small bowl, whisk together the flour, salt, pepper, paprika, and garlic powder. In a separate bowl, combine the egg and milk. Working in batches, coat the scallions in the flour mixture, then the egg mixture, followed by a second coating of the flour mixture. Set the coated scallions on one of the prepared baking sheets.

Heat the olive oil over medium-high heat in a large skillet until the oil smokes. Fry the battered scallions in the hot oil until they are browned and crispy, 5 to 7 minutes. Transfer them to the second prepared baking sheet to drain.

When the casserole has baked for 40 minutes, remove the lid, then bake the casserole uncovered for 15 to 20 minutes, or until the sauce is bubbling and the green beans are tender when tested with a paring knife.

Top the casserole with the scallions, and bake it for 5 to 7 minutes, or until the scallions are golden and set to the casserole. Let the casserole rest, covered, for at least 10 minutes before serving it.

# Prosciutto-Wrapped Asparagus

Effortless and utterly savory, this salty little side dish is the perfect way to enjoy your vegetables! During the days of the prairie, it was rather uncommon to see many dishes made up entirely of vegetables. Even then, meat, potatoes, and freshly baked bread were the foods of choice, as they were simple and filling. However, vegetables were still enjoyed, though in a rather plain fashion. This recipe is a wonderful way to liven up what could be considered an unflavored savory vegetable. Simply wrap strips of prosciutto around sprigs of fresh asparagus, and roast them until the meat is crispy. It's a foolproof side that is wonderful in the spring, when the asparagus is ready for picking.

## SERVES 4

*1 lb (454 g) asparagus, ends trimmed*

*8 oz (226 g) sliced prosciutto, cut in half lengthwise*

*2 tbsp (30 ml) olive oil*

*1 tsp fine sea salt*

*Pinch of freshly cracked black pepper*

*½ cup (50 g) finely grated Parmesan cheese, for serving*

*Flaky sea salt, for serving*

Preheat the oven to 425°F (220°C). Line a baking sheet with parchment paper.

Wrap each piece of asparagus with a slice of prosciutto, and space them evenly on the prepared baking sheet. Drizzle the asparagus with the olive oil, and season it with the salt and pepper.

Roast the asparagus for 10 to 12 minutes, or until the asparagus is tender and easily pierced with a fork. Evenly sprinkle the Parmesan and sea salt over the asparagus before serving.

# COUNTRY BREADS

When I began learning the art of cooking from scratch, one of the first staples that I made an effort to perfect was bread. My mother and I had just moved to the countryside, and we knew few people in the area. We were invited over for a bread-making lesson with a new friend, and it was there that I discovered that the craft was much simpler than I had previously believed. I thought only true bakers—professionals— could make bread, or that you would need special equipment that I did not have. Instead, I watched with wonder as the new friend brought together a loaf in a bowl, kneading and shaping it with care. It rose within the hour, as we sat around chatting and sipping on cups of hot coffee. Soon, the table was graced with a gorgeous whole wheat loaf, and we were amazed!

I have been making bread for almost a decade, and it has become one of the crafts of cookery that I am best at. Since learning how to make that first loaf, I have taught myself to create sandwich breads, crusty artisanal loaves, buns and biscuits, crackers, sourdough, ciabatta, pretzels, challah, pastries, and more. It is an art that I absolutely adore, and I hope that I can continue sharing warm loaves fresh from the oven with my family for the remainder of my life. The beauty of bread making is that there is always room for improvement, and once you have figured out the feel for making bread, any recipe is possible!

In this chapter, you will find an array of beautifully simple breads that one may have found back in the day. Ingredients such as whole wheat flour, hard cider, and even potatoes pop up to create loaves from interesting yet uncomplicated ingredients. Staples such as Potato Sandwich Bread (page 127) and Big Buttermilk Biscuits (page 143) are perfect for the beginner. If you are looking to add something new to your recipe rotation, you might enjoy making a Crusty French Country Boule (page 129) or Salty Hard Cider Soft Pretzels (page 136). Whatever you decide to make first, be prepared to fall in love with the delicious scents and tastes each loaf will bring to your kitchen. This is country bread making.

# Potato Sandwich Bread

For centuries, bakers have been mixing mashed potatoes into their bread dough to create starchy and flavorful loaves. It is, in fact, common knowledge that Martha Washington was famous for making potato rolls at Mount Vernon. She'd mash up Irish potatoes with butter, and mix them into home-ground flour. Breads of this nature were not popularized until the eighteenth century, when wheat was scarce and rather expensive. Potatoes actually make bread a bit lighter in texture and whiter in color. Today, I typically associate potato breads with the Amish and Mennonite bakers in my local community, and I have come to love the flavor and beautiful texture of this bread myself. I find that this recipe makes an ideal sandwich bread, with its close crumb and hardly ever a large air bubble in sight!

## MAKES 2 LOAVES

1½ cups (360 ml) water

1 medium baking potato, peeled and cubed

1 cup (240 ml) buttermilk

3 tbsp (39 g) granulated sugar

2 tbsp (28 g) salted butter

2 tsp (12 g) kosher salt

6–6½ cups (750–813 g) all-purpose flour, divided

2 tbsp (24 g) active dry yeast

In a medium saucepan with a lid, combine the water and potato. Bring the water to a boil over medium-high heat, then lower the heat until the water is at a simmer. Cover the pan, and cook the potato for about 12 minutes, or until it is easily pierced with a fork. Mash the potato in the water with a potato masher, fork, or handheld electric mixer. Do not drain the water. Measure out 1¾ cups (420 ml) of the potato liquid, which will look like soupy mashed potatoes. If there is not enough potato liquid, add more water to the measuring cup to accommodate. If there is still liquid in the pan, discard it.

Transfer the potato liquid from the measuring cup to the pan, then add the buttermilk, sugar, butter, and salt to the saucepan. On an instant-read thermometer, measure the temperature of the mixture. If it's above 120°F (50°C), let it cool until it reaches that temperature; if it's below 120°F (50°C), heat it to that temperature.

In the bowl of a standing electric mixer fitted with a dough hook, add 2 cups (250 g) of the flour and the yeast. Add the potato mixture to the dry ingredients, and beat until it's combined. Slowly begin to incorporate the remaining flour, ½ cup (64 g) at a time, until a firm, elastic dough forms. Knead the dough until it no longer sticks to the sides of the bowl, about 10 minutes. It is better for the dough to be a bit on the wet side than too dry. Alternately, you can make this bread by hand. Mix the ingredients in a similar fashion in a large bowl with a wooden spoon. When a shaggy dough has formed, begin kneading in flour by hand, turning out the dough onto a floured surface. Knead until the dough is smooth, soft, and elastic, about 20 minutes.

*(continued)*

# Potato Sandwich Bread (Continued)

Grease a large bowl lightly with oil or cooking spray. With wet hands and on a lightly floured surface, begin to pull the corners of the dough over itself, stretching and folding, until it creates a smooth ball. Place the dough ball into the bowl, turning it over so both sides are coated in oil, and cover the dough with plastic wrap or a clean, damp towel. Allow the dough to rise in a warm place for 1 hour, or until it's doubled in size.

Deflate the dough by gently pressing down on the center of the dome. Cover it, and let it rest for 10 minutes. Divide the dough into two equal-sized pieces. On a lightly floured surface, roll out half of the dough into an 8 x 10–inch (20 x 25–cm) rectangle. Take the shorter end of the dough and roll it into a jelly roll shape. Press the edge to seal, and pinch the ends closed. Repeat these steps with the other half of the dough.

Grease two 8 x 4–inch (20 x 10–cm) loaf pans. Place the rolled dough into the pans, cover it, and let the dough rise until it nearly doubles in size, 30 to 40 minutes.

Meanwhile, preheat the oven to 375°F (190°C). Bake the loaves for 35 to 40 minutes, or until they are golden brown on top and sound hollow when tapped with your fingertips in their pans. Allow the bread to sit in the pans for 10 minutes, then move them to a wire cooling rack. Let the loaves come to room temperature before slicing them, if you can wait! The bread will keep for 5 to 7 days.

# Crusty French Country Boule

I love making sourdough bread, but it can be rather complicated without fully explaining how sourdough works. I wanted to create a loaf of bread that resembled a sourdough boule, but without all the hassle of working with a sourdough starter. With this recipe, you have almost instant success. This is a classic French-style bread with a crunchy crust that brings out all the things you love about sourdough! For much of the nineteenth century, this style of bread was a staple in rustic kitchens, paired with a bit of cheese and perhaps a slice of tomato or a piece of salt pork. The boule is baked in a Dutch oven, similar to the style of baking bread in an old-fashioned stove.

## MAKES 1 LOAF

1¾ cups (420 ml) warm water

1 tbsp (12 g) active dry yeast

1 tbsp (13 g) granulated sugar

1 tbsp (18 g) sea salt

5 cups (625 g) all-purpose flour

Cornmeal

Lightly grease a bowl and set it aside.

In the bowl of a standing electric mixer fitted with a dough hook or a large bowl, combine the water, yeast, and sugar. Let the mixture rest for about 5 minutes, until the yeast has bloomed, or grown and become bubbly. Whisk in the salt.

With the mixer on medium-low speed, slowly begin to incorporate the flour, 1 cup (125 g) at a time, until a soft and smooth dough forms. Add as much flour as you can until the dough no longer sticks to the sides of the bowl, but is still a bit tacky to the touch. Alternately, you can make this bread by hand. Mix the ingredients in a similar fashion in a large bowl with a wooden spoon. When a shaggy dough has formed, begin kneading in flour by hand, turning out the dough onto a floured surface. Knead until the dough is smooth, soft, and elastic, about 20 minutes.

Shape the dough into a ball and place it in the greased bowl. Cover the dough with a damp towel or plastic wrap, and let it rise until doubled in size, about 1 hour.

Gently deflate the dough with your hands, and turn it out onto a lightly floured surface. Shape the dough into a ball by stretching and pulling the sides of the dough away and underneath the ball. Place the ball of dough in a bread banneton or on top of a piece of parchment paper on the counter; cover the dough with a damp towel or plastic wrap. Let it rise until nearly doubled in size, about 45 minutes.

*(continued)*

# Crusty French Country Boule (Continued)

Meanwhile, preheat the oven to 425°F (220°C). Place a large Dutch oven with a lid in the oven, and preheat it for 25 minutes.

When the Dutch oven is done preheating, remove it from the oven. Sprinkle the bottom with a bit of the cornmeal. Cut a piece of parchment paper to 12 x 16 inches (30 x 40 cm), and place it on the countertop. Carefully flip the risen dough onto the center of the parchment paper, and lift the dough from the banneton. Slash the top of the loaf with a sharp knife or bread lame in any pattern that you wish. I usually make a straight line down the center of the boule, followed by small diagonal cuts, about ½ inch (1.3 cm) long, on either side of the straight line. This makes a beautiful leaf design. With your hands, gently lift the ends of the parchment paper and place the prepared dough in the Dutch oven, over the cornmeal.

Bake the boule, covered, for 35 minutes. Remove the lid of the Dutch oven, then bake the boule for 15 to 20 minutes, or until the crust is a deep golden color and the bread sounds hollow when tapped on with your fingertips. Let the boule rest for at least 1 hour before slicing it.

# Rustic Brown Oatmeal Loaf

This recipe, while called a brown bread for its beautiful dark coloring, is actually a molasses bread. Brown bread, traditionally made with rye flour, became popular in the early 1800s. For this particular recipe, it is a bit of a new take on what some might know as an anadama bread, or one made with cornmeal and molasses, which gives the loaf its brown color and a unique flavor. A much easier recipe to follow, this is a rather humble and hearty loaf, making it a staple to pair alongside a country stew or shepherd's pie.

## MAKES 2 LOAVES

2⅓ cups (560 ml) boiling water

1 cup (90 g) rolled oats, plus more for sprinkling

½ cup (112 g) salted butter, cubed

⅓ cup (80 ml) molasses

1 tbsp (14 g) packed brown sugar

5 tsp (20 g) active dry yeast

2 tsp (12 g) sea salt

5½–6½ cups (688–813 g) all-purpose flour

Lightly grease a large bowl and set it aside. Grease two 8 x 4–inch (20 x 10–cm) loaf pans.

In the bowl of a standing electric mixer fitted with a dough hook, pour the water over the oats. Stir in the butter, molasses, and brown sugar. Let the mixture sit for 6 to 8 minutes, or until an instant-read thermometer registers around 120°F (50°C).

To the oat mixture, add the yeast and salt and stir well. Slowly begin to incorporate the flour, 1 cup (125 g) at a time, until a soft and smooth dough forms. Add as much flour as you can until the dough no longer sticks to the sides of the bowl, but is still a bit tacky to the touch. Place the dough in the greased bowl, and cover it with a damp towel or plastic wrap. Let the dough rise in a warm place until doubled in size, about 60 minutes.

Gently deflate the dough with your hands. Divide the dough into two equal-sized pieces. On a lightly floured surface, roll out half of the dough into an 8 x 10–inch (20 x 25–cm) rectangle. Take the shorter end of the dough, and roll it into a jelly roll shape. Press the edge to seal, and pinch the ends closed. Repeat with the other half of the dough.

Place each shaped loaf into a greased loaf pan. Cover the dough with a damp towel or plastic wrap, and let it rise until nearly doubled in size, 30 to 40 minutes.

Preheat the oven to 375°F (190°C). Brush the tops of the loaves with a bit of water, then sprinkle the tops with rolled oats. Bake the loaves for 35 to 40 minutes, or until the bread has become a deep, rich brown color and sounds hollow when tapped on with your fingertips. Remove the pans from the oven and place them on a wire cooling rack. Let the loaves cook in the pans for 10 minutes before removing them. Cool the loaves to room temperature before slicing them.

# Whole Wheat Bread Bowls

A homemade bread bowl can turn an ordinary soup into something special. The history of serving soup in a bowl made from bread dates all the way back to the thirteenth century. Bread bowls were often a staple for serving heavier soups, such as chowder, in the colonies and during westward expansion. If bread bowls intimidate you, this recipe is absolutely foolproof and incredibly simple to follow. Essentially, you are making a very large dinner roll and hollowing out the middle. Whole wheat flour brings about an extra depth of flavor to the bread.

## MAKES 6 LOAVES

2½ cups (600 ml) warm (110°F [43°C]) water

2 tbsp (24 g) active dry yeast

2 tsp (8 g) granulated sugar

1 tbsp (18 g) fine sea salt

1 cup (120 g) whole wheat flour

5 cups (625 g) all-purpose flour

Egg wash: 1 large egg + 1 tbsp (15 ml) water

Lightly grease a bowl. Grease two baking sheets.

In the bowl of a standing electric mixer fitted with a dough hook, combine the water, yeast, and sugar. Let the mixture sit for about 5 minutes, or until the yeast has activated and become bubbly. When the yeast has bloomed, whisk in the salt. Add the whole wheat flour and begin mixing on low to medium speed for about 2 minutes, or until the flour is well combined. Slowly begin to incorporate the all-purpose flour, 1 cup (125 g) at a time, until a nice, uniform dough forms that no longer sticks to the sides of the bowl. The dough should still be soft and slightly sticky, not stiff. It is better to have a wetter dough than a dry one.

Form the dough into a ball, and place it in the greased bowl. Cover the dough with plastic wrap, a damp towel, or a large plate, and let it proof for about 1 hour, or until doubled in size.

Gently deflate the dough with your hands, and separate it into six equal-sized pieces. Stretch and fold the pieces of dough, pinching the ends underneath, and shaping them into balls. Place the balls on the greased baking sheets, about 4 inches (10 cm) apart, and allow them to rise for 40 to 60 minutes, or until almost doubled.

Meanwhile, preheat the oven to 400°F (200°C). For the egg wash, whisk the egg with the water in a small bowl and set it aside. Once the bread has risen, brush the loaves with the egg wash. Bake the loaves for 35 to 40 minutes, or until golden brown and the bowls sound a bit hollow when tapped on with your fingertips. Allow the loaves to cool to room temperature.

To use the bowls, core out a cylinder of dough from the center using a serrated knife. With your fingers, lightly scrape out any extra bread to create a bowl. You can adjust how much filling you pull out to your liking, but don't take out too much, or your bowl may become soggy from your soup!

# Salty Hard Cider Soft Pretzels

The history of pretzels is extensive and full of symbolic roots. While the origin of the soft pretzel is up for debate, there is plenty of documentation throughout the centuries of its presence in Germany, Austria, and Switzerland. The pretzel traveled across the ocean with Swiss-German immigrants, many of whom who settled in the same community where my family lives today. Soon, delicious, warm pretzels became a staple in rural communities. This recipe creates an old-fashioned-looking soft pretzel, with a dough that is soft, sweet, and moldable. The addition of hard cider brings about a pleasant and robust flavor that I love.

## MAKES 12 PRETZELS

¼ cup (60 ml) warm water

2 tbsp (24 g) active dry yeast

¼ cup (50 g) granulated sugar

12 oz (354 ml) hard apple cider, room temperature

4 tbsp (56 g) salted butter

2 tsp (12 g) kosher salt

5–6 cups (625–750 g) all-purpose flour

½ cup (110 g) baking soda

Pretzel salt, for sprinkling

TIP: Pretzels must be boiled in water with baking soda in it to achieve that incredible deep brown crust. Make sure to boil them for only about 1 minute at most. If they are boiled longer, they may pick up a bit of a metallic taste.

Lightly grease a large bowl and set it aside. In the bowl of a standing electric mixer fitted with a dough hook, combine the water, yeast, and sugar. Let the mixture stand for 5 minutes, or until the yeast blooms, or grows and becomes bubbly.

Add the cider, butter, and salt, and mix to combine the ingredients. Add 2 cups (250 g) of the flour, and begin to knead the dough on medium speed. Slowly incorporate as much of the remaining flour, 1 cup (125 g) at a time, as possible, until a soft dough forms and pulls away from the sides of the bowl. Knead the dough on medium speed for 5 to 8 minutes. The dough should be soft and smooth, but not sticking to your fingers.

Place the dough in the greased bowl. Cover it with a damp kitchen towel and let it rise until doubled in size, about 1 hour. Preheat the oven to 425°F (220°C). Line two baking sheets with parchment paper. In a large Dutch oven or saucepan, bring 2 quarts (2 L) of water to a boil.

Meanwhile, begin shaping the pretzels. Divide the dough into twelve equal-sized pieces. Roll each piece into a long rope, about 20 inches (50 cm) long. Bring the right end of the rope and cross it over the left, forming a fish shape. Cross the ends again and flip it toward the top of the pretzel. Press the ends together gently.

Stir the baking soda into the boiling water. Make sure the baking soda is fully dissolved. Add the pretzels, two at a time, to the boiling water. Boil them for 1 minute, splashing water onto the tops of the pretzels with a spoon. Remove the pretzels from the water with a slotted spoon, and place them on the baking sheets. Sprinkle them with the pretzel salt. Boil and salt the remaining pretzels. Once all the pretzels are boiled, bake the pretzels for 10 to 15 minutes, or until they are dark golden brown and the insides do not look doughy. Serve immediately.

# Pillowy Soft Dinner Rolls

Sweet, soft, and velvety, these dinner rolls are a brioche lover's dream. Rather than sugar, honey makes a delightful sweetener for breads, helping to flavor the dough and to create a dreamy, rich texture to the crumb. These rolls are perfect alongside any supper, and they even make a lovely little base for a miniature sandwich. A meal on the prairie is not truly complete until the hot rolls are served!

## MAKES 12 ROLLS

1 cup (240 ml) warm whole milk

1 tbsp (12 g) active dry yeast

¼ cup (60 ml) honey

1 tsp fine sea salt

4–5 cups (500–625 g) all-purpose flour, divided

3 large eggs, beaten

½ cup (112 g) salted butter, softened

Egg wash: 1 large egg + 1 tbsp (15 ml) water

TIP: You can easily make these rolls ahead of time. Once the rolls have been shaped, cover them with plastic wrap and refrigerate them overnight. Place them on the counter at room temperature for 30 minutes before baking them.

Lightly grease a large bowl and set it aside.

In the bowl of a standing electric mixer fitted with a dough hook, whisk together the milk, yeast, and honey. Let the mixture sit for about 5 minutes, until the yeast has bloomed, or grown and become bubbly. When the yeast has bloomed, add the salt and whisk to combine it.

Next, add 2 cups (250 g) of the flour and the eggs. Begin to knead with the dough hook on low to medium speed until the flour and eggs are well combined with the liquids. Slowly begin incorporating the rest of the flour, 1 cup (125 g) at a time, until a dough begins to form.

Begin to add the butter in pieces, kneading the dough on high speed for about 10 minutes. The dough is ready when it no longer clings to the sides of the bowl. If needed, add more flour. The texture will be smooth and elastic. Place the dough into the greased bowl, and cover it with a damp towel or plastic wrap. Let the dough rise in a warm place until it's doubled in size, about 1 hour.

Meanwhile, grease a 9 x 13–inch (23 x 33–cm) baking dish.

Gently deflate the dough with your hands, and divide it into twelve equal-sized pieces. Shape each of the pieces into a small ball by gently pulling the edges underneath the roll and twisting it around on the counter. Pinch the seams closed. Arrange the rolls in the prepared baking dish. It is OK if they touch each other. Cover the rolls with a damp towel or plastic wrap, and let them rise until nearly doubled in size, 45 to 50 minutes.

Meanwhile, preheat the oven to 350°F (180°C). In a small bowl, whisk together the egg and water for the egg wash. Brush the tops of the rolls with the egg wash. Bake the rolls for 25 to 30 minutes, or until the rolls are golden brown and soft to the touch.

# Fluffy and Sweet Corn Bread

Corn bread has a long history in the American kitchen. Historically, it was a starchy staple made from ground corn mixed with a bit of water and then stewed. The version that we eat today resembles something rather different and much tastier. I personally prefer a corn bread that tastes more like a sweet and soft cake, and that is exactly what this recipe is! There is rarely a meal served at our home without a side dish of homemade corn bread. An American staple, in my opinion, it pairs so well with main courses, such as a bowl of chili, barbecue, meatloaf, fried chicken, and much more. This bread is sweet, fluffy, and should be enjoyed with a dollop of freshly whipped butter and a drizzle of local honey.

### SERVES 6

1 cup (124 g) fine yellow cornmeal

1 cup (125 g) all-purpose flour

4 tsp (18 g) baking powder

⅓ cup (66 g) granulated sugar

1 tsp kosher salt

½ cup (120 ml) whole milk

½ cup (120 ml) buttermilk

1 large egg

¼ cup (60 ml) vegetable oil

1 tsp vanilla extract

Preheat the oven to 400°F (200°C). Grease an 8 x 8–inch (20 x 20–cm) baking dish and set it aside.

In a large bowl, whisk together the cornmeal, flour, baking powder, sugar, and salt. Add the milk, buttermilk, egg, oil, and vanilla. Stir the batter with a wire whisk until the liquids are just combined and the mixture is no longer dry. Spread the batter evenly in the prepared pan.

Bake the corn bread for 30 to 35 minutes, or until a knife inserted into the center comes out clean. Place the pan on a wire cooling rack for 10 minutes before slicing and serving it.

# Big Buttermilk Biscuits

Is there anything more divine than waking up to the smell of fresh, warm biscuits baking in the oven? This is something that I love to do for my children, and I hope it is a memory that they cherish forever. Biscuits are one of my favorite quick breads, simply for the fact that they are, well, quick! Buttery, flaky, and soft, they are a wonderful treat served at the breakfast table with homemade butter and strawberry jam, or topped with savory pork sausage gravy (see page 21). They bring about memories for me as well, and I always feel like I traveled back in time a little bit to when the biscuits may have been baked in a wood-burning stove in a log cabin.

## SERVES 6

4½ cups (563 g) all-purpose flour

4 tsp (18 g) baking powder

1 tsp baking soda

1 tsp fine sea salt

1 cup (224 g) salted butter, cold and cubed

2 cups (480 ml) buttermilk

Preheat the oven to 425°F (220°C).

In a large bowl, whisk together the flour, baking powder, baking soda, and salt. With a pastry blender or fork, cut in the butter until the mixture resembles coarse crumbs, about the size of a pea.

Pour in the buttermilk and mix it in with a wooden spoon until a dough begins to form. Switch to your hands, and knead the mixture until a uniform dough comes together with hardly any dry bits left. It will be a bit lumpy and shaggy. As you are kneading, try to form 7 to 8 layers, folding the dough over onto itself. If your dough no longer feels cold, place it back in the refrigerator for 15 to 20 minutes.

Place the dough on a lightly floured surface. Press it out to about 1 inch (2.5 cm) thick with your hands. With a biscuit cutter or the top of a drinking glass, cut straight down into the dough to form the biscuits. Press the leftover dough pieces together, and repeat this process until all the dough has been used.

Place the cut biscuits on a baking sheet, and bake them for 20 minutes, or until they are golden brown and no longer doughy inside. Serve the biscuits immediately.

TIPS: The secret to making big fluffy biscuits is simple: do not press out your dough too flat. The biscuit's height comes from being cut thickly in a downward motion. It is best not to twist or shake the biscuits as you cut them, and I like to cut mine when the entire piece of dough is around 1 inch (2.5 cm) thick. Another tip? Fold the dough over itself into layers as you form it in the bowl. This creates those delicious, flaky layers during baking.

# Soft and Smooth Amish Noodles

If you have ever made pasta before, you may be aware that to make true Italian noodles, you need only flour and eggs. This recipe, however, is closer to an Amish-style noodle, which uses a fat, such as butter or oil, and liquid, such as water or broth. These noodles are super soft and smooth, and, in my opinion, they are easier to work with than traditional pasta. I love to use them for all sorts of pasta dishes, such as homemade spaghetti, fettuccine, ravioli, and lasagna. I also use them in my Amish Beef and Noodles (page 88) recipe.

## MAKES 1 POUND (454 G) DRIED NOODLES

4 cups (500 g) all-purpose flour

4 large eggs

¼ cup (60 ml) extra virgin olive oil

¾ cups (180 ml) water

Place all the flour in a large bowl. Make a well in the center, and add the eggs, oil, and water. With a fork, mix the ingredients until they begin to form a dough. With your hands, bring the dough together, and knead it until all the dry bits are gone.

Shape the dough into a disk and cover it with plastic wrap. Leave it on the counter for at least 1 hour, or refrigerate it for up to 2 days, until you are ready to use it.

Slice the dough into four equal-sized portions. To shape the dough into noodles, you can either use an electric pasta roller as its manufacturer recommends, or you can roll out the dough by hand.

To roll the dough by hand, roll one portion of dough into a 12 x 16–inch (30 x 40–cm) rectangle. It should be almost paper-thin. Sprinkle both sides of the dough with a bit of flour to prevent it from sticking. Roll up the dough like a jelly roll, starting with the shorter end.

With a sharp knife, slice the rolled pasta into ½-inch (1.3-cm)-wide strips. Unroll the sliced noodles, and place them on a noodle drying rack or a piece of parchment paper. Let them stand until fully dry, 12 to 24 hours. Store the noodles in an airtight container for up to 3 days.

# FROM-SCRATCH
# DESSERTS

Like many home cooks, some of the first from-scratch recipes that I tried making on my own were baked goods. I learned how to bake with my dad, who learned from his mother, who was taught by her mother, and so on. This love that we pass on from family member to family member is remembered in the methodical steps, the whisking of the batter and filling of the cake pans, the scent wafting from the oven, and the first tastes of something sweet on our tongues.

Many of the popular desserts from the pioneer days are made with fresh fruits. This was a way to preserve the summer harvest in a small way throughout the week, though I doubt the treats ever lasted that long. They certainly do not in my home! The wonderful thing about old-fashioned baked goods is that they bring back childhood memories. Prairie Blueberry Slump (page 167), Peach-Swirled Frozen Mascarpone Custard (page 174), and Velvety Molasses Pumpkin Pie (page 178), all make their way into this chapter to remind you of days gone by, when desserts were simple and sweetened with things picked fresh from gardens and orchards.

In this chapter, I share some of my reimagined tried-and-true desserts that you are sure to love. Each is made entirely from scratch, from the dough to the fillings. While they may seem daunting, my goal in the kitchen is to always reduce the steps that it takes to reach a truly delectable dessert. I hope that you enjoy making these rustic and simple sweets for your family!

# TIPS FOR BETTER PIE BAKING

Baking a perfect pie crust can be a tricky business to get into. When I first started making pies, I would often wind up with a crust that had a soggy bottom. While those pies were still entirely edible, I knew that it could be better. After a lot of trial and error, I found some tips and tricks to create a truly delicious pie crust that will leave your family sitting in awe at the supper table. While there is plenty of science behind making pie crust work, I try to pass up the science and to make cooking simpler and more enjoyable for anyone who wants to learn. These tips are meant to ease your anxiety. Learn something new and have fun baking!

## Dough Formation Makes a Difference

When it comes to baking pie crust, keeping things cold is extremely important. To form a perfectly crispy and flaky crust, the fat in your recipe must be kept cold at all times, or you risk having a soft and soggy crust. You may use lard or butter as the fat of choice. Either option works fine, but it is more difficult to work with butter, as it melts more quickly and is susceptible to becoming liquefied in your hands as you knead the dough together. This is why the way you form the dough matters. It is best to use your hands on the dough as little as possible. You may want to try a pastry blender or fork to cut the fat into the flour. I like to use a fork to mix my dough together when it is time to add the water or other liquid. If your dough has become too warm and the butter visually melts, or if the dough is sticking to your fingers or the counter, pop it in the freezer for a few minutes, then resume forming it.

## Blind-Bake Your Crust

Blind-baking means to simply bake the crust without any filling in it. This is an essential step for pies with an unbaked filling, such as a cream pie. Custard pies such as pumpkin, pecan, or quiche also need a partially baked crust to prevent the bottom from becoming a soggy mess. Fruit pies, however, do not require any blind-baking, because they are not as wet as other fillings. To blind-bake, preheat the oven to 425°F (220°C). Pierce the bottom of your crust all over with a fork. This helps to keep the bottom from bubbling up while baking. Place a piece of parchment paper on your crust, then fill it with pie weights. These can be purchased commercially, or you can use a pantry item, such as dried beans. Bake the crust for 15 minutes. Remove the pie weights and parchment paper, then bake the crust for 5 to 10 minutes, or until the crust is lightly browned and the bottom is no longer wet. This entirely depends upon how well baked you want the crust. If you will be using an unbaked pie filling, bake the crust for a full 25 minutes.

## Brush the Entire Crust with an Egg Wash

Before putting your pie filling into the pie shell, brush it all over with an egg wash, a mixture of egg and water. Many pie recipes will tell you to simply brush the crimped edge of the pie. Brushing the entire shell creates a sealed layer between the pie crust and the filling. If you like, before you fill the crust, bake it for a few minutes after the egg wash has been applied. This creates a seal on the crust to prevent it from overbrowning and the bottom from becoming soggy. Using an egg wash also prevents the edges of the crust from burning when the filled pie is baked. I never need a pie shield for the edges of my crust because of this tip!

## *Refrigerate after Each Step*

Limp dough: That was the result after countless attempts at a pretty
crimped edge or a beautiful shape cut from leftover dough to top my
crust. So, I started refrigerating my crust after each step before baking. In
all truth, I usually put my crust and any extra pieces, including cut-outs
or lattice strips, into the freezer for 20 minutes before using them. This
helps to chill the dough quickly, without it becoming fully frozen and
unworkable. If you are shaping the edge of a pie crust, be sure to chill the
crust before baking it. This will ensure that it keeps its shape and won't
soften in the oven.

# Crisp and Flaky Pie Crust

Pie is a Heartland staple and is the most popular of all other desserts at a community potluck. I make pies all year round, and I love that they can fit into every season. In the summer, they are filled with freshly picked berries, in the fall, homegrown pumpkin. I personally love a good custard or cream pie! Whichever type of pie you prefer, this crust has been my utmost favorite of all the different crusts I have worked with over the years. Flaky and slightly sweet, it makes a great backdrop for any filling, sweet or savory. I love using lard for my dough because it creates a really firm and crispy crust. If you like a crust that's softer and has a lot of flavor, you may prefer to use butter.

## MAKES 1 OR 2 (12-INCH [30-CM]) CRUSTS

### Single Pie Crust

1¼ cups (157 g) all-purpose flour

1 tbsp (13 g) granulated sugar

½ tsp fine sea salt

⅓ cup (75 g) lard or butter, cold

3–4 tbsp (45–60 ml) ice cold water

### Double Pie Crust

2 cups (250 g) all-purpose flour

1½ tbsp (20 g) granulated sugar

1 tsp fine sea salt

⅔ cup (150 g) lard or butter, cold

6–8 tbsp (90–120 ml) ice cold water

In a medium bowl, whisk together the flour, sugar, and salt. With a pastry blender or fork, cut in the lard or butter until it forms coarse crumbs about the size of a pea.

Slowly incorporate the water, 1 tablespoon (15 ml) at a time. Begin to mix the crust with a fork until it forms a dough. You may add more or less water, but I find that I need about 3 tablespoons (45 ml) for a single pie crust. The final dough should not be dry, and it should not be sticky and wet. If you are using butter, it will be a bit softer than a dough made with lard.

Form the dough into a disk; form two disks for a double pie crust. Cover the dough with plastic wrap and refrigerate it for at least 1 hour or freeze it for 20 minutes before using it. You may refrigerate the crust for up to 3 days, or freeze it for several months.

 TIP: To make a single pie crust with equal amounts of butter and lard, use 2 tablespoons (28 g) plus 2 teaspoons (8 g) of butter and 2 tablespoons (28 g) plus 2 teaspoons (8 g) of lard. To make a double pie crust with equal amounts of butter and lard, use ⅓ cup (75 g) of butter and ⅓ cup (75 g) of lard.

# Easy Puff Pastry

Puff pastry is a light and flaky dough with several layers of buttery, delicious flavor. It can be used for both sweet and savory dishes, generally as appetizers or desserts, but also as the breading or crust for a main dish. The beauty of this culinary fascination is that it does not require any additional leavening agents, such as yeast or baking powder. The only ingredients needed are flour, salt, and lots of butter! Puff pastry is a French creation; the French discovered that the thin, even layers of butter and dough rise or "puff" during baking, as the moisture in the butter creates steam.

While puff pastry is not entirely difficult to make, it is a long and somewhat tedious process. There are many factors that come into play, such as temperature, timing, evenness of the lamination—or the process of folding and rolling butter into dough—and the correct amounts of flour and butter. I only attempted to make puff pastry myself after several years of baking pie crusts, but I wish that I had tried it sooner. There are many steps, but this recipe and process that I am about to share with you is really quite simple and foolproof! It is much easier to purchase frozen sheets of puff pastry from the grocer, but it is really quite a thing of beauty and pride to make it yourself.

## MAKES 2 PASTRY PORTIONS

*4½ cups (563 g) all-purpose flour*

*1 tsp kosher salt*

*2 cups (448 g) butter, cold and cut into ½-inch (1.3-cm) slices*

*1¼ cups (300 ml) ice water*

In a large bowl, whisk together the flour and salt. Add in the butter, tossing it in the flour mixture until all the sliced pieces are fully coated in flour and separated from each other. It is important that the butter is sliced and *not cubed*.

Pour in the water and begin to stir the mixture with a spoon. It will still be quite dry, but once the water and flour have begun to form a dough, begin to knead the mixture with your hands until a cohesive ball has formed and most of the flour has been incorporated. There may still be some dry bits at the bottom of the bowl, and that is OK.

Remove the dough from the bowl and knead it six times, for 4 to 5 minutes, on the counter. The pieces of butter will still be quite large and whole. Shape the dough into a 6 x 6–inch (15 x 15–cm) square.

Lightly flour the surface of your counter. Roll out the dough to a 12 x 16–inch (30 x 40–cm) rectangle. Fold the dough crosswise into thirds, like an envelope, to form a 12 x 6–inch (30 x 15–cm) rectangle. With the shorter 6-inch (15-cm) end, fold the dough crosswise into thirds again to form a 4 x 6–inch (10 x 15–cm) rectangle. This will create nine layers of folds.

*(continued)*

## Easy Puff Pastry (Continued)

Repeat this rolling and folding process once more, until you end with another 4 x 6–inch (10 x 15–cm) rectangle. Wrap the dough in plastic wrap and chill it for 30 minutes in the refrigerator.

Remove the dough from the refrigerator, and repeat the rolling, folding, and chilling process twice more. Altogether, this will take about an hour of chilling time. To use the dough in a recipe, cut the dough in half. Each half is good for one portion of puff pastry dough for the recipes in this book.

Before baking with the dough, allow at least 30 minutes of chilling before rolling and shaping it as the recipe directs.

# Apple or Peach Cream Cheese Ladder Loaf with Streusel Topping

Growing up, I can remember taking walks with my mom from our old Victorian home down to the little bakery in town. We lived only a few blocks away, so it became a tradition to enjoy a cold chocolate milk and fresh donut as we watched passersby on their way to work. While I loved having a cream-filled donut, one of the pastries I remember most fondly was a braided loaf of bread covered in a streusel topping that we called "coffee cake." This delicious breakfast pastry was not a coffee cake, but rather a version of a braided sweet bread filled with cream cheese.

After having moved away, it was a recipe that I craved and had to re-create at home! This braided bread looks beautiful and slightly complicated, but it is really rather manageable to make. The braiding itself is as simple as cutting the bread into strips and folding them over each other. It has a more bread-like texture than a traditional pastry, giving it an old-fashioned feel. But the best part has to be the delicious streusel crumble topping and warm, sweet fruit inside.

## SERVES 6

### Ladder Loaf

2 tsp (8 g) active dry yeast

2 cups (250 g) all-purpose flour

⅓ cup (80 ml) milk, plus more for brushing

4 tbsp (56 g) salted butter, softened

2 tbsp (26 g) granulated sugar

½ tsp fine sea salt

2 large eggs

For the Ladder Loaf, lightly grease a bowl and set it aside. In the bowl of a standing electric mixer fitted with a dough hook, combine the yeast and the flour. Set it aside.

In a small saucepan over medium heat, warm the milk, butter, sugar, and salt until the mixture is at about 120°F (50°C) on an instant-read thermometer, or the butter has just started to melt. Pour the milk mixture over the flour and yeast mixture. Add the eggs. Stir the mixture on medium speed for about 2 minutes, or until the ingredients are well combined. Knead the dough until it is smooth, 6 to 8 minutes.

Shape the dough into a loose ball and place it in the greased bowl. Cover the bowl with plastic wrap, and refrigerate the dough overnight, about 12 hours.

In the morning, punch down the dough. Let it rest, covered, for 15 minutes. Meanwhile, preheat the oven to 350°F (180°C), and grease a baking sheet.

*(continued)*

# Apple or Peach Cream Cheese Ladder Loaf with Streusel Topping (Continued)

### Apple or Peach Filling
2 tbsp (28 g) packed brown sugar

1 tsp ground cinnamon

¼ tsp ground nutmeg

¼ tsp ground allspice

Pinch of fine sea salt

2 cups (226 g) sliced fresh apples or peaches

4 oz (112 g) cream cheese, softened

2 tbsp (28 g) salted butter, softened and cubed

### Streusel Topping
3 tbsp (24 g) all-purpose flour

3 tbsp (39 g) granulated sugar

Pinch of ground cinnamon

3 tbsp (42 g) salted butter, cold

### Powdered Sugar Icing
1 cup (120 g) powdered sugar, sifted

2–3 tbsp (30–45 ml) whole milk, divided

½ tsp vanilla extract

In a small bowl, make the filling. Combine the brown sugar, cinnamon, nutmeg, allspice, and salt. Stir in the apples.

Roll out the dough to a 12 x 14–inch (30 x 36–cm) rectangle. Transfer the dough to the greased baking sheet. Spread the cream cheese down the center of the dough in a 3-inch (8-cm)-wide strip. Spread the fruit filling down the center of the cream cheese, and top that with the butter.

Make fourteen cuts, 1 inch (2.5 cm) apart, along the long sides of the dough. Begin to alternate folding the strips over the top of the fruit filling, folding them over each other like arms at an angle. Press the ends that meet in the middle together. Cover the dough with plastic wrap or a damp towel, and let it rise until it's nearly doubled in size, about 40 minutes.

While the dough is rising, make the Streusel Topping. In a small bowl, mix together the flour, sugar, and cinnamon. With a fork, cut in the butter, until it resembles coarse crumbs, about the size of a pea.

Brush the dough with a bit of milk and sprinkle the streusel topping over it. Bake the loaf for about 30 minutes, or until the center is no longer doughy and the crust is golden brown.

While the loaf bakes, make the icing. Stir together the sugar, 2 tablespoons (30 ml) of the milk, and the vanilla, until the mixture is the consistency of molasses. Add more milk, if necessary, to get the right consistency.

Serve the loaf warm, drizzled with the icing.

# Miniature Raspberry Almond Galettes

A galette is a type of rustic pastry with an exposed filling and roughly folded edges. They can be baked free-form, or without a pan, and many are. Often, they are served sweet, but they can be savory as well, with a vegetable and cheese filling. Because they do not require a tin or fancy pastry-shaping techniques, they are an easy and accessible dessert for those who are new to pie baking, especially if you need a recipe that is more forgiving. This is a traditional fruit-filled galette with an added hint of sweet almonds. You can make one large galette with this recipe, or turn them into miniature individual desserts, as I do here!

## SERVES 4

*Single Crisp and Flaky Pie Crust (page 151)*

*2 cups (240 g) fresh raspberries*

*2 tbsp (16 g) all-purpose flour*

*4 tbsp (52 g) granulated sugar*

*1 tbsp (15 ml) freshly squeezed lemon juice*

*1 tsp lemon zest*

*Egg wash: 1 large egg + 1 tbsp (15 ml) water*

*6 oz (170 g) almond paste*

*Coarse sugar, for dusting*

*1 tbsp (14 g) salted butter, cubed into 4 pieces*

*Vanilla custard, for serving*

Begin by making the pie dough. Shape it into a disc, wrap it in plastic, and refrigerate it for at least 1 hour, or up to 2 days.

In a medium bowl, gently mix together the raspberries, flour, sugar, lemon juice, and lemon zest. Set aside the mixture.

Preheat the oven to 375°F (190°C). Line two baking sheets with parchment paper and set them aside.

Divide the pastry into four equal-sized pieces. On a lightly floured surface, roll out each piece to be a rough circle about 6 inches (15 cm) in diameter. You may choose to trim around the edges for a perfect edge, or leave them free-form for a rustic look. Place the pie dough circles on the baking sheets, spacing them evenly.

In a small bowl, whisk together the egg and water for the egg wash. Brush the inside of the pie dough circles with the egg wash. Divide the almond paste into four equal-sized pieces. Roll each piece flat, with a rolling pin or with your hand, and place them in the center of the pie dough circle.

Scoop ¼ cup (45 g) of raspberry filling into the center of each circle. Flatten the filling slightly, leaving a 1-inch (2.5-cm) border, so that it is not in a mound.

Starting with one circle, fold the edge of the pie dough up and around the filling in a concentric circle. Leave a bit of the filling exposed. Brush the outer edge of the dough with the egg wash. Sprinkle the edges with the coarse sugar. Place a dab of butter on top of the exposed filling. Repeat with the remaining galettes.

Bake the galettes for 25 to 30 minutes, or until the pie crust is golden and the filling is bubbling. Place the galettes on a wire cooling rack to cool them slightly, then serve them, topped with the vanilla custard.

# Summer Triple Berry Pie

A fruit-filled pie is one of the best kinds of pie to start with, if you are a beginner. Living in the Heartland, which has many native berries for foraging, it seems only fitting that this was often the dessert of choice for families living on the prairie. Throughout the summer months, there are lots of sweet local berries to pick, such as mulberries, aronia berries, blackberries, gooseberries, wild strawberries, and juneberries. The filling is made with ease, as it has no requirement to be cooked beforehand. Simply mix up a big bowl of fruit with sugar, lemon juice, and a little thickener to create an incredible masterpiece. To keep things as old-fashioned as possible, I use simple ingredients, such as butter, egg, and flour, to thicken this pie filling. This pie can be made with any mix of berries, from strawberries to blueberries to blackberries. In the end, you want to have about 4 cups (550 g) worth of berries to fill a 9-inch (23-cm) pie.

## SERVES 6

*Double Crisp and Flaky Pie Crust (page 151)*

*4 cups (550 g) mixed berries, such as blackberries, blueberries, raspberries, or strawberries*

*1 cup (200 g) granulated sugar*

*¼ cup (32 g) all-purpose flour*

*1 tbsp (8 g) cornstarch*

*Pinch of fine sea salt*

*1 large egg*

*1 tsp freshly squeezed lemon juice*

*Egg wash: 1 large egg + 1 tbsp (15 ml) water*

*2 tbsp (28 g) salted butter, cubed*

*Coarse sugar, for dusting*

Prepare your pie crust according to the directions on page 151. Refrigerate each disk for at least 1 hour, or up to 2 days.

Preheat the oven to 400°F (200°C).

When the pie crusts are chilled, remove one from the refrigerator. On a lightly floured surface, roll out the dough into a 12-inch (30-cm)-diameter circle. Trim around the edge. Place the crust in a 9-inch (23-cm) pie plate, pressing down all around the bottom with your fingertips. If needed, trim around the edge so there is 1 inch (2.5 cm) of dough hanging over the edge of the plate. Tuck the edge under, and flute the edges of the crust to your liking. Poke the bottom of the crust all over with the tines of a fork. Refrigerate the crust for at least 1 hour, or until you are ready to use it.

In a large bowl, gently mix together the berries, sugar, flour, cornstarch, salt, egg, and lemon juice with a spatula, so as not to crush the berries.

Remove the chilled pie shell from the fridge. In a small bowl, whisk together the egg and water for the egg wash. Brush the entire shell with the egg wash. Fill the shell with the berry mixture. Dot the filling with pieces of the butter. Set aside the pie.

*(continued)*

# Summer Triple Berry Pie *(Continued)*

With the second chilled disk of pie dough, roll it out to a 12-inch (30-cm) diameter circle. This is where you have some creative freedom with the pie. You may choose to completely cover the entire pie with a solid piece of dough, to cut the dough into lattice strips, or cut out shapes with a cookie cutter. Have fun with it! If your dough has become too warm and the butter visually melts, or if the dough is sticking to your fingers or the counter, refrigerate it for about 20 minutes, then resume forming it.

If you use a full crust to cover the pie, cut at least one slit in the top crust to release steam; if you use a lattice top, leave spaces between the strips for air to escape. Brush the crust all over with the egg wash, then dust it with the coarse sugar.

Bake the pie for 60 minutes, or until the crust is golden brown and the filling is bubbling. If needed, cover the edge of the crust with foil to prevent overbrowning. Let the pie rest for at least 1 hour, to allow the filling to thicken, before slicing it.

# Pioneer Stacked Celebration Cake with Applesauce Filling

A stacked cake, served traditionally, is a pioneer's version of a wedding cake. Each guest of the bride would bring a layer of cake to stack on top of one another, often with an applesauce or apple butter filling, as this was easy enough to make in large quantities. Because most families' supplies were limited, this was an affordable way to create a large cake for celebrating with a small village of guests. It was also common for the stacks to be made with different colors and flavors of cakes, as every person had different ingredients at home. It is said that you would know how popular the bride was among the townsfolk by how many layers of cake she had! This recipe is easily my favorite in the entire cookbook, and the molasses cake alone is to die for!

## SERVES 6

### Molasses Cake
2 cups (250 g) all-purpose flour

½ tsp baking soda

½ tsp baking powder

½ tsp fine sea salt

½ cup (116 g) salted butter, softened

½ cup (100 g) granulated sugar

½ cup (120 ml) blackstrap molasses

2 large eggs

1 cup (240 ml) whole milk

### Buttermilk White Cake
2 cups (250 g) all-purpose flour

1 cup (200 g) granulated sugar

½ tsp baking powder

¼ tsp baking soda

¼ tsp fine sea salt

½ cup (120 ml) buttermilk

½ cup (112 g) salted butter, softened

½ tsp vanilla extract

2 large egg whites

For the cakes, preheat the oven to 375°F (190°C). Grease and flour three 8 x 1½–inch (20 x 4–cm) round cake pans. Set them aside.

For the Molasses Cake: In a large bowl, whisk together the flour, baking soda, baking powder, and salt. In the bowl of a standing electric mixer fitted with a paddle attachment, cream the butter, sugar, and molasses for about 4 minutes, until light and fluffy. Add the eggs, and mix until fully incorporated. Add the flour mixture alternately with the milk, ending with the flour mixture. Scrape the sides of the bowl, and mix until the flour is just combined.

Scoop about 1⅓ cups (320 ml) of the batter into each of the prepared cake pans. It's possible you will have only enough batter to fill two of the cake pans; that's OK. Bake the cakes for 15 to 20 minutes, or until a cake tester or toothpick inserted into the center comes out clean. Let the cakes sit for 10 minutes, then remove them from the pans onto wire racks to cool.

Make the Buttermilk White Cake while the molasses cakes bake. Wash the mixer bowl and paddle attachment. In the mixer, whisk together the flour, sugar, baking powder, baking soda, and salt. Add the buttermilk, butter, and vanilla. Beat on medium to high speed for 2 to 4 minutes, scraping the sides of the bowl occasionally, or until the batter is smooth and has no lumps. Add the egg whites, and beat the batter on high for 2 minutes. Cover the mixer bowl with plastic wrap, and refrigerate the batter until you are ready to use it.

*(continued)*

# Pioneer Stacked Celebration Cake with Applesauce Filling (Continued)

## Chocolate Sour Cream Cake

1½ cups (188 g) all-purpose flour

1½ cups (300 g) granulated sugar

1 cup (88 g) Dutch-process cocoa powder

1½ tsp (8 g) baking soda

1½ tsp (6 g) baking powder

1 tsp fine sea salt

2 large eggs

½ cup (120 ml) buttermilk

½ cup (120 ml) sour cream

½ cup (120 ml) vegetable oil

2 tsp (10 ml) vanilla extract

½ cup (120 ml) black coffee, hot

## Filling and Toppings

48 oz (1.4 L) chunky cinnamon applesauce, divided

Whipped cream

Chopped nuts, such as pecans or walnuts

Edible flowers, such as pansies or violas

 TIP: You can speed up the cooling of the cakes by wrapping each layer in plastic, then refrigerating the layers.

Once the molasses cakes are cooling on the wire racks, clean the cake pans, and grease and flour them. Remove the white cake batter from the fridge, and scoop about 1⅓ cups (320 ml) of the batter into each pan. It's possible you will have only enough batter to fill two of the cake pans; that's OK. Bake the cakes for 15 to 20 minutes, or until a cake tester or toothpick inserted into the center comes out clean. Let the cakes sit for 10 minutes, then remove them from the pans onto wire racks to cool.

Make the Chocolate Sour Cream Cake while the white cakes bake. Wash the mixer bowl and paddle attachment. In the mixer bowl, whisk together the flour, sugar, cocoa powder, baking soda, baking powder, and salt. Add the eggs, buttermilk, sour cream, oil, vanilla, and coffee to the dry ingredients. Beat the mixture until the batter is smooth, 2 to 4 minutes. Cover the mixer bowl with plastic wrap, and refrigerate the batter until you are ready to use it.

Once the white cakes are cooling on the wire racks, clean the cake pans, and grease and flour them. Remove the chocolate cake batter from the fridge, and scoop about 1⅓ cups (320 ml) of the batter into each of the pans. It's possible you will have only enough batter to fill two of the cake pans; that's OK. Bake the cakes for 15 to 20 minutes, or until a cake tester or toothpick inserted into the center comes out clean. Let the cakes sit for 10 minutes, then remove them from the pans onto wire racks to cool.

When the cakes have fully cooled—you should have six to eight very thin layers—assemble the cake on a cake stand or large plate. Begin with a base layer.

For the filling, scoop ¼ cup (60 ml) of the applesauce onto the center of the base layer, then spread it to the edge, leaving about a 1-inch (2.5-cm) border. Stack on the next layer of cake, alternating the flavors, and repeat, filling and stacking until all the layers are used. If your cake becomes too top heavy, gently press toothpicks into the cake to hold the layers together.

Spread a large dollop of the whipped cream over the applesauce on the top layer of the cake. Sprinkle the nuts and flowers over the cream.

# Prairie Blueberry Slump

A *slump* is a dessert in which sweet, soft biscuit dough is dropped on top of a syrupy berry filling and cooked. This dessert has also been called a *grunt*, depending on where you are located. This dish was created in the American colonies because the ingredients and tools needed to create a cobbler were scarce to find. A slump was easily made by dumping everything into a pan and cooking it right over the fire or stove, though I bake mine. Kind of fun, right? In truth, this dessert really is quite a bit of a slump, or lump rather, of sweet, sticky blueberries and delicious warm biscuits. It's perfect served with whipped cream or frozen custard.

## SERVES 6

2 cups (250 g) all-purpose flour

2 cups (400 g) granulated sugar, divided, plus more for sprinkling

4 tsp (18 g) baking powder

1 tsp fine sea salt, divided

4 tbsp (56 g) salted butter, cold and cubed

1 cup (240 ml) whole milk

¼ cup (60 ml) heavy cream

1½ lb (680 g) fresh blueberries

1 cup (240 ml) freshly squeezed orange juice

1 tsp vanilla extract

Whipped cream or frozen custard, for serving

Preheat the oven to 400°F (200°C).

In a large bowl, whisk together the flour, ¼ cup (50 g) of the sugar, baking powder, and ½ teaspoon of the salt. Cut in the butter with a pastry blender or fork, until the mixture forms coarse crumbs, about the size of a pea. Pour in the milk and cream, and stir the ingredients together with a fork or wooden spoon until a dough forms. Cover the dough with plastic wrap and chill it until you are ready to use it.

In a 12-inch (30-cm) cast-iron skillet, combine the remaining 1¾ cups (350 g) of sugar and remaining ½ teaspoon of salt, blueberries, orange juice, and vanilla. Bring the mixture to a boil over medium-high heat, then reduce the heat to a simmer. Simmer the filling for about 10 minutes, or until it has become like a syrup.

Scoop the biscuit dough, ¼ cup (64 g) at a time, on top of the blueberry mixture, randomly dropping the dough until the top is mostly covered. Dust the biscuit dough with sugar. Bake the slump for 30 to 35 minutes, or until the biscuits are golden brown and the filling is thick and bubbly. Serve the slump hot, with the whipped cream.

# Strawberry-Thyme Shortcakes with Whipped Crème Fraîche

Strawberries are ripe and ready to pick in mid- to late June here on the farm. I have so many wonderful memories—most of them involving chubby baby fingers and little chins dribbling with sweet, red juice—around strawberry picking with my children. They are a favorite to munch on as a snack or to use in summery desserts. Strawberry shortcakes are a lovely sweet to make for after lunch or a midafternoon treat. The addition of fresh thyme creates an herbal flavor that feels like your dessert came straight out of the garden. While most strawberry shortcake recipes use plain whipped cream, I love the addition of whipped crème fraîche, which is a version of sour cream with a higher fat content. It is tangy, rich, and thick, which makes it an ideal ingredient to combine with a sweet and syrupy fruit.

## SERVES 8

### Shortcake Biscuits

2 cups (250 g) all-purpose flour

4 tsp (18 g) baking powder

3 tbsp (39 g) granulated sugar

½ tsp fine sea salt

½ cup (112 g) salted butter, cold and cut into ½-inch (1.3-cm) cubes

⅓ cup (80 ml) buttermilk

⅓ cup (80 ml) heavy cream, plus more for brushing

1 tbsp (14 g) turbinado or coarse sugar, for sprinkling

For the biscuits, preheat the oven to 425°F (220°C). Line a baking sheet with parchment paper. Put the bowl of an electric stand mixer in the refrigerator.

In a large bowl, combine the flour, baking powder, sugar, and salt. Cut in the butter with a pastry blender or fork until the mixture forms coarse crumbs, about the size of a pea. Stir in the buttermilk and cream with a wooden spoon, until a shaggy dough forms, 2 to 4 minutes.

Gently knead the dough, using your hands, until there are no longer any dry bits remaining in the bowl. On a lightly floured surface, evenly press out the dough to about a ½ inch (1.3 cm) thickness. With a 3-inch (8-cm) round biscuit cutter, cut straight down into the dough to cut eight shortcakes. You may have to gather the dough back together, press the dough into a ½ inch (1.3 cm) thickness, and cut shortcakes a couple of times to make eight cakes.

Place the shortcakes on the lined baking sheet. Brush them with heavy cream, then sprinkle the tops with the turbinado sugar. Bake the shortcakes for about 16 minutes, or until they are golden brown on top and no longer raw in the middle. Set aside the shortcakes.

*(continued)*

# Strawberry-Thyme Shortcakes with Whipped Crème Fraîche (Continued)

## Whipped Crème Fraîche
1 cup (240 ml) heavy cream

1 cup (240 ml) crème fraîche

¼ cup (30 g) powdered sugar

1 tsp vanilla extract

## Strawberry Filling
2 cups (332 g) sliced strawberries

¼ cup (50 g) granulated sugar

1 tbsp (2 g) fresh thyme leaves

Next, make the Whipped Crème Fraîche. Put the chilled bowl on the electric stand mixer, and add the heavy cream, crème fraîche, and powdered sugar. Whip the ingredients, using the whisk attachment, until stiff peaks form, 4 to 6 minutes. Stiff peaks are formed when a peak holds itself up and retains its shape when you lift the whisk from the cream. Stir in the vanilla. Chill the Whipped Crème Fraîche until you are ready to assemble the cakes.

For the filling, in a medium bowl, mix together the strawberries, sugar, and thyme. Let the strawberries stand for 15 to 30 minutes to macerate, or begin to release some water and become syrupy.

To assemble the cakes, slice the shortcake biscuits in half. Top the bottom half of the shortcakes with some of the Strawberry Filling and Whipped Crème Fraîche. Close the shortcakes with the top half of the biscuit. Serve the shortcakes cold.

# Chocolate Buttermilk Cake with Mocha Buttercream and Chocolate Ganache

A true pioneer's cake, this recipe is made with melted bittersweet chocolate rather than unsweetened cocoa powder. Chocolate was not as accessible then as it is now, easily found in the aisles of your nearest supermarket. It arrived in bricks to little country general stores, and it was rather bitter tasting, so many cooks mixed it with sugar and milk to sweeten the flavor. This cake has a lovely spongy texture and light chocolaty flavor, which is only enhanced by the dreamy mocha buttercream and rich chocolate ganache. It is my favorite for serving as a birthday cake, though I also love it as an afternoon sweet to pair with a dark roast coffee or espresso.

SERVES 6

### Chocolate Buttermilk Cake
2 cups (250 g) all-purpose flour

2 cups (400 g) granulated sugar

1 tsp baking powder

1 tsp baking soda

¼ tsp fine sea salt

1⅓ cups (320 ml) buttermilk

½ cup (112 g) salted butter, softened

1 tsp vanilla extract

2 large eggs

3 oz (88 ml) melted bittersweet chocolate

### Mocha Buttercream Frosting
½ cup (112 g) salted butter, softened

2 oz (60 ml) melted bittersweet chocolate

¼ cup (60 ml) buttermilk, plus more as needed

¼ cup (60 ml) strong black coffee, cooled

1 tsp vanilla extract

2–3 cups (240–360 g) powdered sugar, divided

For the cake, preheat the oven to 350°F (180°C). Grease and flour two 9-inch (23-cm) round cake pans. Set them aside.

In the bowl of a standing electric mixer fitted with a paddle attachment, whisk the flour, sugar, baking powder, baking soda, and salt. Add the buttermilk, butter, vanilla, eggs, and chocolate. Beat the batter on high speed for 2 to 4 minutes, or until the ingredients are just combined. Scrape the sides of the bowl, and beat the batter again to fully incorporate the ingredients.

Pour the batter into the prepared cake pans, about halfway full. Bake the cake for 35 minutes, or until a toothpick inserted into the center comes out clean. Cool the cakes in the pans for 10 minutes, then transfer them to wire cooling racks. Let the cakes cool completely before decorating them.

Make the frosting. In a large bowl, cream the butter with a handheld electric mixer for 2 minutes, or until it's soft and creamy. Add the chocolate, buttermilk, coffee, vanilla, and 2 cups (240 g) of the powdered sugar. Beat for 2 to 3 minutes, or until the frosting is thick and stiff. Add more powdered sugar if you like thicker frosting, or more buttermilk if you prefer it thinner. Set aside the frosting, or refrigerate it until you are ready to use it.

*(continued)*

# Chocolate Buttermilk Cake with Mocha Buttercream and Chocolate Ganache (Continued)

## Chocolate Ganache

8 oz (226 g) semisweet chocolate, chopped finely

½ cup (120 ml) heavy cream

¼ cup (26 g) shaved chocolate, for decorating

Next, make the ganache. Place the semisweet chocolate in a heatproof bowl. Heat the cream in a small saucepan over medium heat on the stove for 3 to 4 minutes, until it begins to gently simmer around the edges of the pan. Pour the hot cream over the chocolate, and cover the bowl with a plate. Let the mixture sit for about 5 minutes, until the chocolate is softened.

With a spatula, mix together the chocolate and cream until they are blended evenly and the chocolate is no longer chunky. Cover the bowl with plastic wrap, and place it in the refrigerator for 1 hour, stirring it every 20 minutes, so that it cools evenly. Once fully cooled, the ganache should be nice and thick.

Assemble the cake. Place one layer of cake, bottom side up, on a cake stand or cake plate. With a spatula, spread frosting all over the top, starting in the middle and working your way to the edge. Place the second layer of cake on top, with the bottom facing up, and spread frosting evenly over the top and down the sides. Pour the cooled ganache over the cake and let it drip down the sides. Top the cake with the shaved chocolate.

# Peach-Swirled Frozen Mascarpone Custard

I love making frozen custard in the summer! Richer and creamier than ice cream, custard is a mixture of egg yolks and heavy cream that is heated over the stove until it thickens. It makes a wonderful chilled dessert, but I like to churn mine into a frozen treat that can be served alongside a warm slice of pie or a heavily frosted birthday cake. This recipe is made extra creamy with the addition of mascarpone, an Italian-style cream cheese that adds just the right amount of tang to such a sweet dessert. You can swirl this with any type of jam, but I think peach makes the perfect addition for a late summer delicacy.

SERVES 6

5 large egg yolks

1 cup (200 g) granulated sugar

1¼ cups (300 ml) heavy cream

1 cup (240 ml) whole milk

1 cup (240 g) mascarpone

1 tbsp (15 ml) vanilla extract

8 oz (226 g) peach jam or preserves

In a small bowl, whisk together the egg yolks and sugar until fluffy, 5 to 6 minutes. Set aside the bowl.

In a large pot, heat the cream and milk until the mixture is just simmering, about 140°F (60°C) on an instant-read thermometer. Remove the pan from the heat.

Pour about ¼ cup (60 ml) of hot cream into the egg mixture, whisking constantly to prevent the cream from cooking the eggs too quickly. Pour the egg mixture back into the pan of hot cream, whisking as you pour. Return the pot to medium heat, and whisk the custard for 5 to 7 minutes, or until it's thickened. The custard should be thick enough to coat the back of a spoon when it's done. Slowly whisk in the mascarpone.

Remove the pot from the heat, and stir in the vanilla. Pour the hot custard into a large bowl and press a piece of plastic wrap directly onto the surface of the custard, to prevent a skin from forming. Refrigerate the mixture for several hours, or until it's fully chilled, 37°F (3°C).

In an ice cream maker, churn the chilled custard for 20 minutes, or until it resembles the consistency of soft-serve ice cream. Transfer the custard to a loaf pan, and swirl in the peach jam with a rubber or silicone spatula. Cover the loaf pan with plastic wrap, and freeze the custard for at least 1 hour before serving. The custard can be frozen for up to 2 weeks.

# Classic Yellow Cake with Lemon Buttercream Frosting

My family loves this classic yellow cake that is so named for the color given by the gloriously rich egg yolks on our farm that turn the cake yellow. It is perfect for birthdays, anniversaries, and all other kinds of spring or summertime celebrations. The tangy and sweet lemon buttercream is delightful during the warmer months! This cake is creamed differently from most cakes, with the butter being incorporated before dissolving the sugar. I have found that this results in a uniform crumb and a springy cake.

## SERVES 6

### Classic Yellow Cake

3 cups (375 g) all-purpose flour

2 cups (400 g) granulated sugar

1 tbsp (14 g) baking powder

½ tsp fine sea salt

1½ cups (360 ml) buttermilk

½ cup (112 g) salted butter, softened

2 tsp (10 ml) vanilla extract

2 large eggs

### Lemon Buttercream Frosting

⅓ cup (75 g) salted butter, softened

4½ cups (540 g) sifted powdered sugar, plus more as needed

¼ cup (60 ml) whole milk, plus more as needed

1 tsp vanilla extract

1 tbsp (15 ml) freshly squeezed lemon juice

Zest of 1 lemon

Fresh blueberries or strawberries, for topping

Fresh lemon slices, for topping

For the cake, preheat the oven to 375°F (190°C). Grease and flour two 9-inch (23-cm) round cake pans. Set them aside.

In a large bowl, stir together the flour, sugar, baking powder, and salt. Add the buttermilk, butter, and vanilla. Mix with an electric mixer on medium speed until the ingredients are just combined and there are no longer any dry bits in the bowl. Scrape the sides of the bowl. Add the eggs, and beat the batter for 2 minutes.

Pour the cake batter evenly into the prepared cake pans, about halfway full. Bake the cakes for 30 to 35 minutes, or until a toothpick inserted into the centers comes out clean. Allow the cakes to cool for 15 minutes in the pans, then transfer them to wire cooling racks. Let the cakes cool completely before frosting them.

For the frosting, in a medium bowl, cream the butter with an electric mixer on medium-high speed until it's soft, 2 to 4 minutes. Add the sugar, milk, vanilla, lemon juice, and lemon zest, and beat the mixture for 2 minutes on medium speed, until it's thick. Add more powdered sugar if you like thicker frosting, or milk if you like thinner frosting.

Assemble the cake. Place one layer of cake, bottom side up, on a cake stand or cake plate. With a spatula, spread frosting all over the top, starting in the middle and working your way to the edge. Place the second layer of cake on top, with the bottom facing up, and spread frosting evenly over the top and down the sides. For serving, top the cake with the blueberries and lemon slices.

# Velvety Molasses Pumpkin Pie

A true pioneer's pie was sweetened with molasses rather than cane sugar. In fact, most recipes you will find from the eighteenth and into the early nineteenth centuries used molasses as a way to flavor and sweeten dishes, often those involving winter squash, such as butternut, acorn, Hubbard, and even pumpkins. True molasses is made from the extracted juice of sugarcane, and it was an import to the American colonies from the West Indies. Refined sugar did not become popular until the 1880s. Today, you may find that it is more expensive to purchase molasses than refined sugar. For a historically flavored pumpkin pie, I think this recipe is wonderfully unique. With a combination of both blackstrap molasses and brown sugar, it will not alter the flavor too much while also giving you a taste of the past.

## SERVES 6

Single Crisp and Flaky Pie Crust (page 151)

½ cup (112 g) packed brown sugar

2 tbsp (16 g) all-purpose flour

½ tsp ground cinnamon

¼ tsp ground nutmeg

¼ tsp ground ginger

¼ tsp fine sea salt

½ cup (120 ml) blackstrap molasses

1 cup (240 ml) whole milk

4 large eggs

1 tsp vanilla extract

2 cups (490 ml) pumpkin puree

4 tbsp (60 ml) melted salted butter

Egg wash: 1 large egg + 1 tbsp (15 ml) water

Whipped cream, for serving

Preheat the oven to 350°F (180°C). Make the pie crust ahead of time, and partially blind-bake it for about 15 minutes, or until the crust is lightly browned. For more information about blind-baking pie crust, please refer to the instructions on page 148.

In a large bowl, whisk together the brown sugar, flour, cinnamon, nutmeg, ginger, and salt. Add the molasses, milk, eggs, and vanilla, and beat for 2 to 3 minutes, until the ingredients are well combined. Stir in the pumpkin and butter.

In a small bowl, whisk together the egg and water for the egg wash. Brush the entire pie shell with the egg wash. Pour in the pumpkin filling.

Bake the pie for 50 to 60 minutes, or until the filling is set and a bit wobbly in the center, and the crust is golden brown. Cool the pie to room temperature before slicing it. For serving, top it with the whipped cream.

# Maple Crinkle-Top Brownies

The secret to brownies with a crinkly, crusty top is in the eggs. Whisking the eggs for several minutes before incorporating them into your batter creates air bubbles that result in a delightfully crinkled top crust. These brownies are a family favorite, and a dessert that I love making in a pinch on winter evenings when I have forgotten to prepare a more time-consuming sweet. They are perfectly gooey and thick. I love serving these brownies warm in a bowl, topped with a few tablespoons of cold milk, a treat best enjoyed when you are wrapped in an old quilt near the woodstove while a winter storm rolls in.

SERVES 9

½ cup (63 g) all-purpose flour

¼ cup (22 g) Dutch-process cocoa powder

1 cup (200 g) granulated sugar

½ tsp fine sea salt

½ cup (120 ml) melted salted butter

1 tbsp (15 ml) vegetable oil

¼ cup (60 ml) maple syrup

2 tsp (10 ml) vanilla extract

¼ cup (60 ml) melted semisweet chocolate

3 large eggs

Powdered sugar, for dusting

Preheat the oven to 350°F (180°C). Grease and flour a 9 x 9–inch (23 x 23–cm) baking pan.

In a large bowl, sift together the flour, cocoa, sugar, and salt. With a whisk, mix in the butter, oil, maple syrup, and vanilla. Stir in the chocolate.

In a small bowl, whip the eggs until they are bright yellow and foaming, 4 to 6 minutes.

Whisk the whipped eggs into the brownie batter for 3 to 4 minutes, until they are well incorporated.

Pour the brownie batter into the prepared baking pan. Bake the brownies for 40 to 45 minutes. For fudgy brownies, bake until a toothpick inserted into the center has some crumbs on it. For more cake-like brownies, bake until the toothpick comes out clean. Allow the brownies to sit for a few minutes, then dust with the powdered sugar and slice them.

# Colonial Custard Bread Pudding with Raisins

One of the best ways to be creative in the kitchen is to create dishes from previous meals, as did cooks of old. If you are ever left with stale bread in your home, which hardly ever happens for me, a good way to make use of the leftovers is by baking up a delicious bread pudding. One of my favorite ways to create a rich, creamy bread pudding is by baking it in a custard sauce. Add some cinnamon and raisins, and I am a happy woman! This bread pudding uses a bit of brandy, a typical addition to many colonial-style baked goods, to spice things up. Once your family gets hold of a piece of this dessert, you will find it won't last more than a day!

## SERVES 12

### Bread Pudding
16 oz (454 g) loaf day-old French bread, cut into 1-inch (2.5-cm) cubes

2 cups (480 ml) heavy cream

2 cups (480 ml) whole milk

1 cup (224 g) salted butter

1 cup (240 ml) brandy

8 large egg yolks

3 cups (600 g) granulated sugar

1 tsp ground cinnamon

½ tsp ground nutmeg

1 tbsp (15 ml) vanilla extract

1 cup (149 g) raisins

### Powdered Sugar Icing
2 cups (240 g) powdered sugar

3–4 tbsp (45–60 ml) whole milk, divided

1 tsp vanilla extract

For the Bread Pudding, preheat the oven to 350°F (180°C). Check the bread for dryness; if it is still moist, spread the cubes evenly on a baking sheet and cook them for about 10 minutes in the oven, or until they are lightly toasted. Grease a 9 x 13–inch (23 x 33–cm) baking dish. Place the bread in the baking dish and set it aside.

In a large pot, heat the cream and milk over medium heat for 5 to 6 minutes, until it just simmers. Add the butter and brandy, then remove the pan from the heat.

In a medium bowl, whisk together the egg yolks and sugar for 5 to 6 minutes, or until fluffy. Pour about ½ cup (120 ml) of the hot cream into the egg mixture, whisking constantly. Transfer the egg mixture back into the pot of hot cream, whisking as you pour, until it's fully incorporated. Return the pot to the heat, and stir in the cinnamon, nutmeg, vanilla, and raisins. Cook the mixture over medium heat for 5 to 7 minutes, or until the custard has thickened and coats the back of a spoon. Remove the pan from the heat.

Pour the hot custard over the bread, and spread it evenly throughout. Bake the bread pudding for 40 to 45 minutes, or until a knife inserted into the center comes out clean.

Make the icing while the bread pudding cooks. In a small bowl, whisk together the powdered sugar, 3 tablespoons (45 ml) of the milk, and the vanilla for about 2 minutes, or until it is thick like molasses. If necessary, add more milk.

Cut the bread pudding into twelve pieces. For serving, drizzle it with the icing. Leftover bread pudding can be refrigerated in an airtight container for up to 4 days. Warm it up for an excellent breakfast choice on a chilly winter day!

# Giant Pioneer Snickerdoodles

A recipe of German or Dutch descent, the snickerdoodle has been around since the late nineteenth century. It is no wonder that these cookies have been around for more than 200 years: they are soft and buttery sugar cookies rolled in cinnamon sugar! While I doubt many pioneers trekked through the American west with snickerdoodles packed in their lunch sacks, I can only imagine that they would have been an incredible delicacy for a weary traveler. A good snickerdoodle is soft and pillowy, and this one has a uniform and chewy texture, which works perfectly for such a gigantic cookie!

## MAKES 12 COOKIES

*3 cups (375 g) all-purpose flour*

*1½ tsp (5 g) cream of tartar*

*1 tsp baking soda*

*2 tsp (6 g) ground cinnamon, divided*

*¼ tsp ground nutmeg*

*½ tsp fine sea salt*

*1¾ cups (350 g) granulated sugar, divided*

*1 cup (224 g) salted butter, just softened*

*2 large eggs, room temperature*

*2 tsp (10 ml) vanilla extract*

Preheat the oven to 375°F (190°C). Set aside two large ungreased baking sheets.

In the bowl of a standing electric mixer fitted with a paddle attachment, whisk together the flour, cream of tartar, baking soda, 1 teaspoon of the cinnamon, nutmeg, salt, and 1½ cups (300 g) of the sugar. Add the butter, and mix on low speed to incorporate it. Increase the speed to medium, and beat until the butter is fully incorporated into the flour mixture, 4 to 5 minutes. Add the eggs, and mix on medium speed for 2 to 4 minutes, until they are fully incorporated into the dough. Add the vanilla, and mix for a minute or so, or until the dough it formed and the ingredients are fully mixed together. Scrape down the sides of the bowl, if needed.

In a small bowl, combine the remaining ¼ cup (50 g) of sugar and remaining 1 teaspoon of cinnamon.

Roll ¼ cup (72 g) of dough into a uniform ball. Coat the cookie dough in the cinnamon sugar mixture, then slightly flatten it on a baking sheet. Repeat with the remaining dough, placing six cookies, about 3 inches (8 cm) apart, on each baking sheet.

Bake the cookies for 14 to 16 minutes, or until the edges are lightly golden brown and the center of the cookie is soft but set. Remove the cookies from the oven, and lightly tap the baking sheets on the counter to help flatten the cookies. Let the cookies bake on the baking sheets for 5 minutes, then move them to a wire rack to cool completely.

# ACKNOWLEDGMENTS

Thank you to my editors, Emily Taylor and Ari Smolin, who reached out to me with an idea for a cookbook. Without you, this project never would have surfaced, and I would have been left questioning if this was the right path for me. This cookbook changed everything about my business and career, and I truly owe that change of pace to you! Thank you for answering my endless supply of questions, for bouncing around ideas and concepts with me, and for always seeing the vision. I truly appreciate everything that you both helped with!

Thank you to Page Street Publishing for helping to create a cookbook that I absolutely adore, for believing in me, and for trusting that this book would be a good fit for the shelves. Thank you to Dianne Cutillo, Laura Benton, and Rosie Stewart. You brought this book to life and out into the world, and I will be forever grateful to you.

To my husband, who never once faltered or questioned the madness involved in writing a cookbook in less than a year. Thank you for believing in me, for helping me find all the dishes and equipment needed to make every photo, for being the absolute best father to our children, and for being my number one cheerleader. You make my life so special every day that you are in it, and you will always be my favorite person to cook for. I love you; I love you; I love you.

To my children: Without your patience and understanding, this book may have never happened. To Tad, thank you for inspiring me to begin this journey and to begin cooking. You inspire me every single day. To Dean, thank you for making me laugh when all seemed lost, for all the snuggles when my mind needed rest, and for trying all the food that I made for this book. To Felicity, who grew in my belly for the entire writing and photography process of this book, thank you for pushing me to go farther than I ever thought I could. I love you all. And thank you to all the snacks that fed and entertained my children while I wrote this book.

Thank you to my parents, without whom I would have never started. You believed in me before anyone else, when my life was a big mystery and when I was at my lowest. Thank you for trusting me to follow my own path to happiness, for the endless late nights and weekend babysitting, and for welcoming my family into your home to create a home of our own. To my dad, thank you for igniting my love of cooking, for listening to all my doubts and troubles, and for washing a seemingly never-ending pile of dishes. To my mom, thank you for being the best business partner, for inspiring me and pushing me to reach farther, and for reminding me that the only person who can hold me back is myself. You are my best friends, and I love you.

Thank you to my readers, who have supported my dreams from the first day I started posting my thoughts and ideas online. You are the reason that this cookbook began, and I cannot ever thank you enough for that. To all the people who read my blog and social media, thank you for continually supporting me. This cookbook is for you, and I hope that it will be one that is used so often that the pages are wrinkled and dog-eared and covered in splashes of ingredients as you cook with it.

# ABOUT THE AUTHOR

Kayla Lobermeier is an author, blogger, recipe developer, photographer, homesteader, and co-owner of the brand Under A Tin Roof with her mother, Jill Haupt. She lives in rural Iowa with her husband, children, and parents on their multigenerational family farm. Under A Tin Roof is a small flower farm and online lifestyle company focused on sharing the joy of seasonal, slow living with others who enjoy gardening, preserving, and cooking with wholesome ingredients. Kayla has been sharing her family's journey into a simpler and sustainable lifestyle for almost a decade, and she has been featured in publications such as *Willow and Sage* magazine, *Where Women Cook*, *Heirloom Gardener*, *Folk* magazine, *In Her Garden*, *Beekman 1802 Almanac*, and *Gardenista*. She has taught cooking and gardening lessons through Kirkwood Community College and has hosted farm-to-table suppers at her family farm. You can usually find her sipping on a hot cup of coffee, reading up on the domestic lives of the Victorians, and snuggling with barn cats. Visit Kayla at underatinroof.com or on Instagram and YouTube @underatinroof.

# INDEX